GOLDING

LORD OF
THE FLIES

NOTES

COLES EDITORIAL BOARD

Bound to stay open

Publisher's Note

Otabind (Ota-bind). This book has been bound using the patented Otabind process. You can open this book at any page, gently run your finger down the spine, and the pages will lie flat.

ABOUT COLES NOTES

COLES NOTES have been an indispensible aid to students on five continents since 1948.

COLES NOTES are available for a wide range of individual literary works. Clear, concise explanations and insights are provided along with interesting interpretations and evaluations.

Proper use of COLES NOTES will allow the student to pay greater attention to lectures and spend less time taking notes. This will result in a broader understanding of the work being studied and will free the student for increased participation in discussions.

COLES NOTES are an invaluable aid for review and exam preparation as well as an invitation to explore different interpretive paths.

COLES NOTES are written by experts in their fields. It should be noted that any literary judgement expressed herein is just that — the judgement of one school of thought. Interpretations that diverge from, or totally disagree with any criticism may be equally valid.

COLES NOTES are designed to supplement the text and are not intended as a substitute for reading the text itself. Use of the NOTES will serve not only to clarify the work being studied, but should enhance the reader's enjoyment of the topic.

ISBN 0-7740-3295-2

© COPYRIGHT 1995 AND PUBLISHED BY
COLES PUBLISHING COMPANY
TORONTO—CANADA
PRINTED IN CANADA

Manufactured by Webcom Limited
Cover finish: Webcom's Exclusive **Duracoat**

CONTENTS

Page No.

William Golding: Life and Works 1
Introduction to *Lord of the Flies* 4
Plot Summary 9
Characters in the Novel 10
Chapter by Chapter Summaries and Commentaries
    CHAPTER 1...................................... 11
    CHAPTER 2...................................... 14
    CHAPTER 3...................................... 17
    CHAPTER 4...................................... 19
    CHAPTER 5...................................... 22
    CHAPTER 6...................................... 24
    CHAPTER 7...................................... 26
    CHAPTER 8...................................... 28
    CHAPTER 9...................................... 32
    CHAPTER 10..................................... 35
    CHAPTER 11..................................... 37
    CHAPTER 12..................................... 39

Structure 42
    Chart: Guide by Chapter to Main Action and
        Location 48
    Questions and Answers on Structure 49

Characterization 53
    Character Delineation Chart 57
    Character Sketches 58
    Questions and Answers on Characters 63

Meaning 68
    Questions and Answers on Meaning 71

Style 78
    Questions and Answers on Style 81

Golding's Technique 89
Review of Criticism 99
Bibliography 107

William Golding: Life and Works

William Gerald Golding was born in Cornwall, England on September 19, 1911. His father, Alec Golding, was a schoolmaster and his mother, Mildred Golding, was an active worker on behalf of women's suffrage and other causes.

Golding's parents encouraged him toward science as an educational pursuit but, in his second year at Brasenose College, Oxford, young Golding shifted his educational emphasis to literature. Today, he also admits to a fondness of archaeology, but it is rather a highly sophisticated knowledge of anthropology that crops up in his first two novels.

Golding's first published work was a slim volume of poetry, which appeared shortly after his graduation from Oxford in 1934. He claims to have "wasted the next four years." When World War II began, he joined the Royal Navy in which he served with distinction for over five years. During this service, Golding had a variety of experiences, highlighted by his participation in the D-Day invasion of France. When Golding was discharged from the Navy at the war's end, he held the rank of lieutenant. There is no question that Golding's experiences in the Royal Navy were the most decisive of his life, particularly in his development as a writer.

After the war, Golding settled down to the peaceful pursuits of teaching and writing. *Lord of the Flies*, his first novel, appeared in 1954, when he was 43. The book was received enthusiastically by most reviewers and E.M. Forster, dean of living English novelists, chose it as the outstanding novel of the year. Readers saw it as a forcefully stated allegory about the evil inherent in the human heart.

This highly successful first novel was followed the next year, 1955, by *The Inheritors*. Golding's second and favorite novel has a theme similar to *Lord of the Flies*. It is a rather esoteric account, written in a simple, direct prose, of prehistoric men who think and communicate with one another by means of visual images. Thematically, the book is a companion novel to *Lord of the Flies*, but its limited range of action and unusual subject are simply not to everyone's taste. As a result, the second novel lies virtually ignored compared to the swell of popularity enjoyed by *Lord of the Flies*, which has

1

sold well over one million copies and has been made into a motion picture.

Both *Lord of the Flies* and *The Inheritors* give clear evidence of Golding's pessimistic view of man's nature and his fate. As Golding told an interviewer at the New York *Herald Tribune*, World War II made a tremendous impression upon him: the war was overwhelming evidence that the evil in man could not easily be explained away. Golding said that he had personally seen "... a hell of a lot in the war that can't be accounted for except on the basis of original evil." He went on to say that he believes that man is born evil and is destined to remain evil.

Golding's third novel, *Pincher Martin*, published in 1956, tells of a naval officer floating in the Atlantic Ocean after his ship has been struck by a torpedo. The officer washes up onto a barren rock, where he eventually loses his mind and dies.

In 1958, Golding completed a play, *Brass Butterfly*. The next year saw the publication of his fourth novel, *Free Fall*. Its protagonist, Samuel Mountjoy, is imprisoned by the Nazis and is awaiting torture in what is colloquially known in most prisons as "the black hole." Mountjoy dwells on the events of his past, much as Pincher Martin did in the watery wasteland of the Atlantic. Golding takes us inside the minds of his solitary characters by way of the literary technique known as the interior monologue. In 1964, Golding published *The Spire*, whose protagonist, the dean of a cathedral, devotes himself to the erection of a great spire, which is criticized by others as a folly. This was followed by *The Hot Gates and Other Occasional Pieces* (1965) and *The Pyramid* (1967).

The Scorpion God, which appeared in 1971, is a collection of three long stories, each set in a totally different historical period (ancient Egypt, prehistory and the Roman Empire). Golding's seventh full-length novel, *Darkness Visible*, published in 1979, deals with the subject of entropy — a theory that deals with the tendency of the universe moving toward increasing disorder. John Thompson wrote in the New York *Times Book Review*:

> Many novelists now write fables, allegories, fantasies, extravaganzas. Golding, though, is all by himself. *Darkness Visible* is magic. Its author cannot

be made to figure in a current ranking. Is he better than this one or that? No, he is different, this wizard.

Critics, in general, are hard put to discern any major trends in Golding's development. Stanley Edgar Hyman has summed it up best, perhaps, by describing Golding as "...the most maverick novelist publishing today. He chooses the least promising fictional subjects and pursues them with a stubborn integrity."

Golding's personal life has been a quiet and a stable one. At present, he is living in Wiltshire, England with his wife, the former Ann Brookfield, whom he married in 1939. They have two children, a son and a daughter. Golding now spends all of his working time at writing, the financial success of his novels having enabled him to relinquish his teaching post.

3

Ansan K.

Introduction to *Lord of the Flies*

Ever since Daniel Defoe wrote *Robinson Crusoe* (1719), landing his hero on a desert island, literature has abounded in stories of castaways. Famous among these are Swift's *Gulliver's Travels*, Jules Verne's *The Mysterious Island* and J.D. Wyss' *The Swiss Family Robinson*.

The immediate source of *Lord of the Flies* was a novel published in 1857, by R.M. Ballantyne: *The Coral Island*. In this book, three English boys are stranded, away from the care of adults, on an island in the South Seas. The boys, somewhat older than in Golding's book, have similar names. In *The Coral Island*, Jack is 18, Ralph (the narrator) is 15 and Peterkin Gay is 13. In *Lord of the Flies*, Ralph is about 12 or 13, as is Jack, while Simon is perhaps a year or two younger. Simon is related by name to the biblical Simon Peter, and here we see a connection with the Peterkin of Ballantyne's book. Actually, however, Piggy seems to resemble Peterkin Gay more than Simon, for Peterkin, like Piggy, is "different" from the other boys. The boys in Ballantyne's book are all very proper British subjects who take upon themselves the task of turning their island into a miniature model of their mother country. They are clean-living optimists, dwelling on what they regard as a South Sea paradise. There is no thought whatsoever that these boys will fail to maintain their British middle-class standards; it would be unthinkable for them to show signs of degenerating. They are very brave and they attack their problems the way adults would. Ballantyne, in a sense, is beating the drum for Great Britain as an empire builder and advancing the rather nationalistic prejudice that Britons have greater courage, higher morals and loftier goals than lesser mortals. The book is, of course, highly romantic. Golding makes no secret of the fact that he has Ballantyne's book in mind. In Chapter 2 of *Lord of the Flies*, Ralph speaks of the exciting prospect of the boys having a whole island to themselves without adult supervision. Then, at the end of Chapter 12, when the naval officer rescues Ralph and questions him about the boys' adventures, Ballantyne's book, *The Coral Island*, is again mentioned. Golding can assume that these references will be meaningful to his readers.

Evil exists in Ballantyne's novel, but is not attributable to the boys. The island is invaded by warlike pirates who, at one point, capture Ralph. Cannibal tribes battle on the shores of the island. But the pirates are all killed and the cannibals are converted to Christianity, whereupon they become eaters of pig, instead of each other. Ballantyne's book is Christian in attitude. His boys are all devout, and the pointed moral is that Christianity disperses the forces of evil in the world. One cannot be a Christian and be evil, so it follows that everyone should become a Christian. Here, Golding differs sharply with Ballantyne, for his choir boys, with their crosses on their cloaks, become the most bloodthirsty of hunters. Once they remove their cloaks they also cast off their religion and give no subsequent indication that Christianity has had any effect at all upon their characters. We can see everywhere in Golding a belief that our social and religious institutions have failed, and that man is really alone with no one and nothing he can turn to for salvation, except himself.

The World of *Lord of the Flies*

As we read the words of a book, we become absorbed in their meanings and the actions they describe. Then, we start to visualize the characters, what they look like, how they talk and behave. We begin to imagine what the setting looks like and the story begins to come alive for us. At this point, we have entered the world of words; we are taking the words on paper for real life. When our reading is interrupted, we suddenly leave this world the writer has created for us and return to our own. As we think about what we have read we begin, almost unconsciously sometimes, to compare the world we know from our personal experiences with the world the writer has been able to suggest to us with his words. If we find the world of the book filled with people who do not talk or act in the ways we are used to in the real world, we may decide the characters are unbelievable. If, on the other hand, the characters even remotely resemble people we have known or read of, we say that they are realistic. Similarly, if the situations the characters are in are entirely beyond any experience we have ever heard of, we will probably find the plot unbelievable. But if the situations *could* occur, we will probably accept them as realistic. In *Lord of the Flies*, we can show that the characters are quite believable, and that their experiences are at least possible. The boys talk like boys; they do not talk like heroes out of fairy tales. They are not impossibly brave, but only as brave as necessity makes them. They are no cleaner than boys can be when no soap is available. Their hair is shaggy. They like to play but don't like to work. They are not very responsible. Even the biggest of them is afraid of the dark. As their stay on the island lengthens, they tend to forget their old civilized ways until, in adapting to their new way of life, they slowly become savages.

As for the plot, we know that a plane could not drop its passenger tube and land the boys safely, because no such plane now exists. Nor is a worldwide atomic war in progress. But these factors do not make the plot unbelievable. We know that a third world war is possible. After all, there have been two already, why could there not be a third? And we realize that, in the future, passenger planes may very well be designed so that in case of trouble a safety device, such as Golding's passenger tube, might be available. And, certainly, we have no trouble believing that people can be marooned on uninhabited islands, for historically this has happened. So, if we recognize that the action of *Lord of the Flies* takes place in some future time, we are able to accept the basic situation as possible.

The modern world of atomic power, supersonic airplanes and the threat of war provides the background for *Lord of the Flies*. We should never lose sight of this world when reading the book, for the adventures on the island are intended to form a comparison with our world. The time of the story has been moved forward into the unknown future. The action takes place on a coral island in the South Seas. This island forms a tiny "world" in itself. So there is the "world" of the island, which is within the "world" the boys come from and return to, a world which is engaged in global warfare. And, of course, there is the world that we know, and against which we compare *Lord of the Flies*.

At first glance, the island seems to be like a paradise. Fruit and flowers are growing together on the trees. No one has to work to eat, since all that is required is that the fruit be picked off the trees and eaten. But there are many indications that the island is not really a paradise. Unlike the Garden of Eden described in the Old Testament, or even the island Ballantyne describes in *The Coral Island*, the fruit of Golding's island is

6

often green, and — green or ripe — it gives the boys diarrhea. They all suffer throughout the book from this complaint. Certainly, this is not very much like paradise. Also, we know that Golding's island is torn at times by fierce tropical storms that uproot whole trees. Again, this does not seem like paradise. And the coconuts are described as "skull-like." Skulls suggest death and, of course, there was no death in Eden. The island *appears* to be like a garden of Eden, but look closer and you discover that it is crawling with flies; sharp thorns on the bushes tear the flesh; rot and decay are everywhere visible. Powerful storms pour down sheets of rain for days at a time, and tear up the beautiful scenery.

The action ranges over three main areas of the island: the central section, low and covered with forest growth; a mountain at one end, where the boys try to maintain a signal fire and where they see the "beast;" and, at the other end of the island, a grouping of coral rock connected by a narrow shelf to the main island. This last resembles a castle and is used toward the end of the book as a rude fortress.

The island world of *Lord of the Flies* is shaped by two characters, Ralph and Jack, who represent opposing forces in the world of the book, as well as in the real world. Ralph's is the civilized world, centering in the safety of the seashore with its comfortable lagoon and its outpost in the mountain, where a signal fire is maintained. Jack's is the hunter's world, and becomes increasingly wild and savage. The forest and the far side of the island with its sheer cliffs, unknown to Ralph, are familiar to Jack. As he achieves power, the action shifts from the abandoned mountain top and the almost abandoned seashore to the rock fortress at the other end of the island.

As we have indicated, *Lord of the Flies* is written in the form of a parable. That is, its characters and plot exist not just to make believable "real-life" situations, but also to form a commentary on the real world. When we see Ralph struggling to hold an orderly civil society together and Jack struggling to wrest power away from him, we are reminded that in the real world a battle is being waged constantly between democratic societies and dictatorships. Democratic societies hold to the belief that every man is entitled to personal freedom of thought and action, while dictators seek to establish the police state: a society wherein the individual is told that he is not important as an individual, but only as he contributes to making his country the most powerful on earth. By the end of *Lord of the Flies*, the boys have managed to destroy their world. It is no longer livable. The fires they have set have destroyed all the trees and all of the fruit. The pigs are either destroyed or will starve, since there is nothing left for them to eat. The island has been rendered barren. In contrast, the real world is very fertile, as we know, but we also realize that if the great nations of the earth ever were to engage in an atomic war, the population of the world would be largely destroyed. The survivors would probably die agonizing deaths of radiation poisoning. The earth itself would become barren, incapable of growth. Eventually, all life would cease to exist. Golding's parable is a grim warning of what mankind must guard against if the human race is to survive.

Plot Summary

During an atomic war, an aircraft carrying a group of about 30 pre-adolescent boys crashes on an uninhabited coral island in the Pacific. The crew has been killed, and the boys are left on their own. They begin to collect themselves into a society of food gatherers under their elected chief, Ralph. A routine of duties is arranged and, at first, the boys live amicably.

Soon, however, differences arise as to their priorities. The smaller children lose interest in their tasks; the older boys want to spend more time hunting than carrying out more routine duties, such as stoking the fire and building shelters. A rumor spreads that a "beast" is lurking in the forest and the children have nightmares.

Jack, promising to fulfil the children's desire for a reversion to primitivism, is chosen as the new chief, and the society splits into two sections: those who hunt and who become savages, and those who believe in rational conduct. Ralph gradually finds himself an outcast, and in the end the army of hunters tracks him down on orders from Jack. Just as Ralph is about to be killed by the "savages," a naval officer arrives with a rescue party.

Characters in the Novel

RALPH: A fair-skinned boy with blond hair, who organizes the marooned boys. He is elected their leader but is not forceful enough to maintain his position. He eventually loses all support and is reduced to the status of an outlaw who must flee for his life.

JACK MERRIDEW: A thin, tall boy with red hair, light blue eyes and freckles. His appearance is cadaverlike and he is physically symbolic of death. He progresses from leader of a choir group to the tyrannical ruler of the island community.

PIGGY: An overweight, asthmatic boy, who cannot see without eyeglasses. He is a wise counsellor and supports Ralph in parliamentary rule. He is subsequently murdered by Roger, who rolls a boulder down upon him.

ROGER: A slight, furtive boy with an inner intensity. He is secretive and quiet. His sadistic nature is revealed when he delights in spearing the mother pig. He later murders Piggy and carries a stake on which to impale Ralph's head.

SIMON: A dark, mystical boy, whom the other boys regard as odd. He is physically weak and prone to hallucination. He often seeks solitude in the forest and, on returning one night, he is mistaken for "the beast" and is beaten to death.

SAM AND ERIC: The twins. They are often slurringly referred to as "Samneric" and are not distinguishable as individuals. They remain with Ralph and Piggy until Piggy's death, when they are captured and forced into Jack's camp.

THE PARACHUTED FIGURE: A dead man who had dropped out of the sky and landed on the mountain. In their few glimpses of him, the boys regard him as the "beast."

THE OFFICER: The only adult in the novel, who appears at the end and saves Ralph from certain death at Jack's hands.

PHIL: A "littl'un" who tells the assembly of his nightmare about "twisty things in the trees."

PERCIVAL: A "littl'un" who becomes hysterical when trying to tell the assembly about "the beast from the sea."

"LITTL'UNS": A group of unnamed boys ranging in age from five to seven years. They are largely ignored by the older boys.

Chapter by Chapter Summaries and Commentaries

CHAPTER 1

The Sound of the Shell

Summary

Two boys encounter each other on a sandy beach between a lagoon and the jungle. One of them, Ralph, is handsome, lean and athletic. The other, Piggy, is fat, asthmatic and wears eyeglasses. Neither of them was acquainted with each other before this moment, and Ralph is unresponsive to Piggy's overtures of friendship. Through their conversation it is revealed that they were being transported somewhere by air along with a number of other children, when their plane crashed after having been attacked. The boys discuss their predicament. Piggy is concerned with locating any other survivors and making a concerted effort to organize them until they are rescued. Ralph is less upset by their problem and, apparently, is not yet fully aware of its seriousness. Unlike Piggy, he is enchanted by the beauty and mystery of their surroundings and is not frightened by the thought of a world temporarily without grown-ups. While wandering near the water, the boys discover a large conch shell. Piggy explains its use as a trumpet. At his prodding, Ralph blows the conch and summons all the other boys to a meeting on the beach.

A large number of boys, in various states of disarray, and ranging in age from about five to near twelve, eventually straggle onto the beach in answer to Ralph's call. Piggy busily devotes himself to learning everyone's name. A boys' choir dressed in black capes and caps, led by Jack Merridew, also comes to the meeting, marching in strict military formation. Jack is an aggressive and stern boy who immediately asserts his authority and takes a place alongside Ralph.

The boys discuss their situation and determine that since no adults are present, it will be necessary to elect a leader. Ralph is chosen, primarily because of his initiative in calling the meeting, much to Jack's disappointment. In order to mend Jack's hurt feelings, Ralph assigns him and his choir the

11

honorable duty of being soldiers and hunters for the group. Jack's pride is restored by this and he further comforts himself by bullying Piggy. Piggy is upset when Ralph reveals his uncomplimentary nickname to the group. Ralph has a sudden realization that he has been inconsiderate. He attempts to apologize to Piggy by behaving to him in a more friendly manner.

After warning the boys to remain near the site of the meeting, Ralph sets out with Jack and Simon, another choir member, to explore the island and to determine whether it is inhabited. Their expedition is an exciting and happy one. They climb hills together and frolic through the exotic jungle, playing games and developing a deep rapport with one another. After a while, they come upon and pursue a young wild pig. Jack prepares to kill it with his knife, but all three boys are secretly horrified by the idea of actually carrying out such a brutal act, and he is unable to stab the helpless animal. After the pig escapes, Jack covers his shame by stating that the animal had moved away too quickly. He asserts that the next time he will not hesitate.

Commentary

A remote jungle setting is useful to the author who wants to avoid the complexities of civilized society and focus instead on simple issues. Similarly, the advantage of using children as characters is that they are, supposedly, innocent and unsophisticated human beings who make no attempt to hide their true selves. It is ironic that while Golding does focus on such fundamental themes as the conflict of good and evil and the passage from innocence to experience, he discovers in this lonely island many of the complex problems that afflict society in the great cities of the world. The cruelty with which the boys taunt Piggy for his fatness, his glasses, and his lack of physical dexterity is like the attitude of sophisticated society to the outsider. Pride, pretence, and jealousy are other adult faults that lurk beneath the innocent appearances of the boys.

In addition to these flaws, the boys contain elements of the nobility and heroism that have made positive contributions to the progress of Western civilization. Simon represents a mystic, Piggy an intellectual and Ralph a political hope for the lost boys. These leaders, along with the wielder of physical

Anson

power, Jack, are faced with the same problems of survival as those of Defoe's Robinson Crusoe on his island. They must organize their lives to meet the threat to survival. Their problems contribute to suspense. Will they be able to make contact with other human beings? Will they be able to keep their group intact? And, more immediately, will they be able to find food and shelter?

The island, with a scar cut across it, is a replica of the cities scarred by atomic warfare. That the atmosphere of violence should extend to this remote region is an indication of Golding's belief in the universality of evil.

The conch shell becomes a symbol of authority. The large, spiral-shaped sea shell, its geometrical form created over a period of scores of years, is a fitting substitute on the island for the slowly evolved laws of human society. In Greek mythology, Triton, the son of Neptune, uses the conch shell to stir or calm the seas. Here, Ralph, following the instructions of Piggy, uses the shell to subdue and control the animal spirits of the boys, at least for a short time.

The mountain signifies many things for many people, but generally represents the dignity of man as he aspires to spiritual freedom. To achieve the top of the mountain is to destroy fear and superstition and to gain mastery over nature.

Rock is a symbol of brute force. When Jack discovers a loose boulder while ascending the mountain, Ralph and Simon help him pry it loose. When the rock plummets down, "the forest further down shook as with the passage of an enraged monster." "Wacco," shouts one boy. "Like a bomb!" cries another. With this episode, the realm of childish innocence of games and slang is broken by the intrusion of a destructive force. It is Jack who distracts the boys from their purpose of climbing the mountain and, for no reason except to create a make-believe "monster" or "bomb," causes them to release this violence. Jack's identity is here established. He is a leader who, like reckless leaders in the civilized world, prefers destruction to creation.

CHAPTER 2

Fire on the Mountain

Summary

When the explorers return, a meeting is called. Ralph explains to the boys that the island is deserted, but that there is plenty of fruit and other food. All that is required, he says, is for them to remain calm and they will eventually be rescued. Until then, the island has enough to keep them well and healthy. Jack once again asserts that he and his army of hunters will keep them supplied with meat.

A semblance of order must be maintained, Ralph continues, and some basic rules must be established for the common good. Jack is excited by the idea of creating many regulations and punishing offenders. For the time being, though, just one rule is made. Ralph announces that only those who are holding the conch will be permitted to speak at meetings. All others must remain quiet until they are recognized.

Piggy lectures the boys on their inattentiveness to the gravity of their problems, and on their most important need, which is, of course, being rescued. Unfortunately, no one pays much attention to this advice, and the group enjoys itself by mocking him. One of the youngest children then shyly tells about a beast he saw the night before. The older boys assure the "littl'un" that it was only a nightmare, but the seeds of doubt and fear are planted even among them.

Ralph discusses the need for building and maintaining a signal fire on the mountain in case a ship or plane passes. The boys enthusiastically pick up on this idea and disorganizedly dash to the hilltop, leaving the meeting in a state of pandemonium. Only Ralph and Piggy remain. Piggy disgustedly comments on the immaturity of the other boys. Ralph rushes off to join the others and Piggy slowly and laboriously follows.

On the mountain the children mill about in confusion, making a huge pile of dead wood. It is discovered that there are no matches and that no one knows how to make a fire, but Jack roughly snatches Piggy's spectacles from the near-sighted boy's face. Using the lenses as a magnifying glass, he soon starts the tinder smouldering and before long a vast fire is raging out of control. The boys flee in terror as the whole hilltop blazes. Afterwards, the group gathers again. Piggy criticizes Ralph for allowing such a senseless and dangerous thing to take place. He again lectures the boys on the proper course of action required for survival and criticizes them for their frivolous behavior. The boys continue to mock Piggy and refuse to heed his warnings. He points out to them that one of the littl'uns has not been seen since the fire went out of control and may perhaps have been burned to death as a result of their irresponsibility. Shame and confusion spread among the boys as they realize the truth of this accusation, but they are unwilling to admit openly any possibility of this accident.

Commentary

The chapter begins in an attempt at order, with Ralph and Jack forming two branches of government. Ralph would make rules for the better conduct of the community's business. Jack, whose choir boys have now become "hunters," would happily enforce the rules by beating up anyone who disobeyed.

With the establishment of a competitive relationship between the legislative and the military, the traditional conflict between civil and military authorities is prepared for.

Golding indicates the falseness of the optimism of the boys. When Ralph promises the boys a good time, "like in a book," the boys shout titles of adventure stories, including *Coral Island*, a novel by R.M. Ballantyne, which for generations has been a favorite of English schoolboys. It tells of three boys on a desert island who survive through courage and cleverness. Ballantyne's characters, Ralph, the quiet, intelligent narrator, Jack, the dashing hero, and the merry Peterkin are models for Golding's leading characters, with both Piggy and Simon deriving from Peterkin. But, of course, Golding is ridiculing the easy solutions of the adventure story. Similarly, when Ralph promises that the boys will be rescued because the queen has a room containing maps of all the islands of the world, he betrays his ignorance. He does not know that there are thousands of unmapped islands. He does not know that the queen is a mere figurehead. His appeal to authority, to the grown-up world of father, navy and queen is in keeping with his storybook attitude to life. By the end of the chapter, the false appearance of orderliness has been shattered. The movement from order to chaos is the pattern of the whole book and of most of the chapters.

The platform, raised above the danger and confusion of the jungle, and shaded comfortably, is an ideal location for parliamentary discourse. It represents a more rational level of human existence. In general, Golding uses imagery of height to represent some kind of human aspiration or mastery.

The snake, like the scar cut across the island by the "passenger tube" and like the rock dropped from the mountain, is an intrusion of the monstrous into the jungle paradise. Later, we will learn that the snake is necessarily present wherever there are human beings, because the snake, as a representation of evil, is part of man. This snake reminds us of another snake in another paradise. The author of *Genesis*, the first book of the Bible, describes the entrance of the Devil, in the form of a snake, into the Garden of Eden with the subsequent fall of Adam into sin. The snake that intrudes here is not the Devil, but represents a similar threat of evil. It injects fear and confusion into the precariously balanced world of the boys. It is a symbol, then, of the forces of disorder threatening society.

Fire often appears in opposition to the snake. The snake is a reminder of the limits of man. Sliding under rocks and through slime, it suggests the dark places of human experience. Fire is usually a symbol of the best in man. It represents the hopes of the human spirit as it flickers upward. For Ralph, who instigates the making of the fire, it represents a faith in society. He is confident of rescue because he believes that society still exists and that society takes an interest in him. In ancient Greek mythology, Prometheus, the son of a Titan, gave man fire. Ralph, in his eagerness to bring fire to the boys, is a modern Prometheus. When the fire rages out of control, it represents a different meaning. Piggy appropriately compares the fire at the end of the chapter to the fire of hell. What began as a co-operative effort has degenerated into a chaos of competitive bickering. Rational control was insufficient to withstand the impulses of the movement. If the leaders had been able to make use of Piggy's wisdom, they might have achieved some stability. But they are too reckless and unthinking. They are too interested in a momentary splurge of firelight, rather than the steady glow of reason, and the result is a destructive conflagration.

Piggy's glasses, which are snatched by the boys to light a fire, are representative of his intellectualism. He might be occasionally useful to the boys, but he will never have their respect. The author, by the way, has made a mistake in having the boys use Piggy's glasses to start a fire. The prescription for Piggy's myopia would be a concave lens, which scatters rather than concentrates the rays of light on a single point.

To enforce the idea of evil lurking amid innocence, Golding uses a "running image," that is, a picture repeated several times in different places in the novel and usually acquiring symbolic significance. Here, the creeper, or jungle vine, is a "running image." On the first page of the novel, Piggy is almost unable to move because he is tangled in creepers. Going up the mountain, the boys have difficulty getting through the creepers. When the small boy tells of the snake, one of the others suggests that it was only the creepers. In the fire that burns at the end of Chapter 2, a tree explodes and creepers shoot into the air. The little boys scream: "Snakes! Snakes! Look at the snakes!" The creepers suggest the same power of disorder present in the snake and released in the ravaging fire. They represent whatever impedes the progress of reason.

CHAPTER 3

Huts on the Beach

Summary
Jack silently stalks a pig through the jungle, but the animal manages to evade him. He returns to the beach where he finds Ralph and Simon hard at work building a hut. Two other huts have already been erected. Most of the other boys are swimming in the lagoon or have rambled off in other directions.

Ralph complains to Jack that most of the boys are unwilling to help in any important project. They enjoy the discussions at meetings and grow enthusiastic about new ideas for a short time. After a while, however, they lose interest in any constructive activity and wander away to play or eat or sleep. He hints that Jack and the hunters would be better employed in building huts than in roaming the jungle. Jack insists indignantly that hunting is necessary and that it is irrelevant that no pigs have yet been killed. Each of the boys tries to explain his feelings and beliefs to the other, but they are unable to express themselves articulately. Resentment swells up between them for an instant, but they are able to control themselves. Finally the two boys go swimming together, baffled by their inability to communicate and trying to stifle their recent feelings of intense dislike for each other. Afterwards, Ralph continues working on the hut and Jack returns to the hunt.

Meanwhile, Simon wanders off into the jungle by himself. After helping some of the littl'uns to get fruit from trees they cannot reach, he continues walking until he is certain that he is alone. He sits quietly beneath a screen of bushes and foliage, staring in awe at the amazing variety of living things — plants, trees, flowers, insects, birds — around him.

Commentary

The different purposes of the boys draw them apart, weakening the unity of the island society. Jack indulges his hunting instinct. Ralph accepts the responsibility of building housing for the boys. Simon finds fulfillment in a natural cell in the jungle. The society is also threatened by a demoralizing fear. The littl'uns scream in the night in terror of the snake-thing. And Jack admits that, at times when he is hunting, he senses something behind him in the jungle hunting him. Both fears are manifestations of a power within the boys that can destroy them. The dark terrors of the jungle reflect the dark parts of the human mind.

Notice, especially in this chapter, Golding's use of point of view — the outlook that an author assumes in narrating a story. An author may select a character who refers to himself as "I" to tell the story. If so, the author must confine himself to things seen, heard, felt and thought by that "I." Depending on whether the narrator is the main character or some minor character, this point of view is called "first-person pro-tagonist" or "first-person witness." A story may be told by an author who looks at everything from the point of view of one character who is referred to as *he* or is identified by a proper name. This is the "third person" or "limited omniscient author" point of view. Or an author may allow himself to go into anyone's mind and to make what editorial comments he likes. This is the "omniscient author" point of view. This is Golding's point of view. Although he differs from some omniscient authors, for example, Dickens, in that he seldom makes comments of his own, but rather chooses to see events through the eyes of his characters, he allows himself the omniscient author's freedom to move from person to person. Thus, in this chapter, he is able to explore the thicket with Jack, report the conversation on the beach between Ralph, Simon and Jack, and finally, follow Simon on his solitary pilgrimage. Read the chapter closely, notice how he observes the actions of Jack and the dialogue of the boys mostly from the outside, and then goes inside the mind of Simon in the jungle, seeing, hearing and feeling the same things that he does. We tend to respond more sympathetically to a character whose mind we enter.

The huts that Ralph is constructing are necessary for survival. But, although in adventure stories the hero is able to whip together sturdy shelters of palm leaves, such huts are actually difficult architectural projects, requiring more than the haphazard efforts of adventuresome boys. The collapsing of the hut represents the failure of civilization on the island.

CHAPTER 4

Painted Faces and Long Hair

Summary

The boys soon become accustomed to the daily rhythm of life on their tropical island. Each morning, the bright sun rises and the air is fresh and sweet. It is the best time of the day and they soon forget their hopes and worries. At noon, the sun reaches a high point in the sky; its heat and light become unbearable. The boys take shelter in the shade and often nap. All during the afternoon they are confused by illusions caused by the sun's white light, and only Piggy recognizes these as mirages. In late afternoon, it grows cool again and then darkness drops quickly upon the island. In this sudden blackness, barely pierced by the stars, they grow restless and frightened.

The smallest boys, known as the littl'uns, lead a life distinct from that of the older ones. They huddle in small groups and spend most of the day eating immense quantities of fruit from the jungle, regardless of its degree of ripeness. As a result, they suffer from chronic diarrhea. They cry often and play occasionally, in small groups. One of the littl'uns, Percival, once stayed in a hut for two days, refusing to eat or speak, and weeping incessantly. The games of these small boys are serious but not happy, as if they are seeking a means of escape from their troubles.

A typical example of some littl'uns at play is described. A few of the older boys, led by Jack, interrupt their game and trample the sand castle. Another of the older boys, Roger, teases the littl'uns by tossing stones at them, but the old taboos of civilized life still dominate him, and he purposely aims to miss. Afterwards, Jack, Roger and the other hunters paint their faces with colored clay. They are excited and pleased by the savage new masks and decide to go hunting again. Their weapons are Jack's knife and some sharpened sticks.

Later on, Ralph and Piggy lie on the beach while the other boys are swimming. Suddenly, they notice a ship on the horizon and discover to their horror that the signal fire on the mountain has gone out. They and the other boys rush to the hilltop and rekindle the blaze, but it is too late. They realize that Jack and the hunters, who are responsible for the maintenance of the fire, have wandered off and abandoned it.

Just at that moment, they see the hunters returning, led by Jack. The boys are chanting a warlike song and carrying the carcass of a dead pig. They are all covered with blood and gore, and have an air of triumph. Ralph informs Jack of the results of his irresponsibility, but he and the other boys are so aglow at their success that they will not listen to the charges. The killing of a pig seems to them a more weighty matter than the routine duty of keeping up a fire, even though this is their only chance for rescue. They chatter in nervous, half-crazed excitement about the hunt, the kill and especially the blood. Piggy also criticizes the hunters, and Jack viciously slaps him, breaking one lens of his glasses. Ralph's dislike for Jack grows even stronger at this example of cruelty. Ralph scolds Jack again and finally the leader of the hunters relents sufficiently to admit that the fire should be kept alive. He apologizes for this act, but has no sorrow for his bullying of Piggy. Most of the boys consider this more than ample compensation for his mistake, for no one except Ralph and Piggy seems to have any real comprehension, even now, of the seriousness of their position on the island, and the need for organization and self-discipline in order to survive.

The pig is roasted and a great feast is held. Jack refuses to give any meat to Piggy, whom he hates deeply, but Simon shares his portion with the helpless, weaker boy. Jack tries to explain the joy and exultation of killing to Ralph, then he joins the other hunters in a wild, barbaric dance around the dwindling fire. The young savages sing and re-enact the hunt. Ralph watches them for a while and then announces that he is calling a meeting. He walks down the hill alone.

Commentary

The smashing of the sand castle is a manifestation of the violence that can become the rule of the island. The older boys, instead of aiding the young, crush their castles, and with them their dreams of kings, queens and noble knights. The older boys are not yet completely uncivilized though. Maurice feels guilty and runs away. Roger, when he pursues one of the littl'uns, is unable to throw rocks directly at him because the laws of school, church and home restrain him. To throw rocks at a fellow human being is to return to an age when the law of survival was the only law governing brute man. Yet, under the layers of civilization, in the English schoolboy throbs the same instinct to kill that flourished in prehistoric times. And, with the nourishing of this instinct, the civilization of the boys fails. The signal fire is allowed to die. A chance of rescue is lost. The energies of the boys are channelled into the one activity of hunting.

As the primitivism of the boys becomes more prevalent, as Jack turns on his fellow human being, Piggy, the cause of rationality seems doomed. The leadership of Ralph gives way to that of Jack. Ralph's success depends on his sensible response to the advice of Piggy and on his ability to make his image of the romantic hero attractive to the boys. If the boys

21

become a tribe of frenzied savages, they will find the civilized manner of Ralph antagonistic. At the end of the chapter, he calls a meeting to stave off Jack's threat to his leadership. But will the rules of parliamentary procedure be sufficient to check a revolution?

The pig dance is a symbol of the new way of life that is replacing the organized society of Ralph. The hunters have finally made their first kill. Beneath the excitement and jubilation runs an undercurrent of fear at the enormity of the deed. As if to compensate for the fear, there is the beginning of a primitive ritual designed to protect the individual from self-consciousness. The chants and ceremonial ring are like the mask worn by Jack to lose his identity. The details of the ritual allow the boys to forget themselves and to become killers.

CHAPTER 5

Beast From the Water

Summary

Walking alone by the water, Ralph is lost in a maze of confusing thoughts. Every semblance of discipline and organization is falling apart. This assembly, he decides, must be a serious one, and things must be accomplished, otherwise there is no hope for them. The boys gather at the usual meeting place and Ralph takes his seat.

Ralph lectures the boys sternly on their immature failure to support any of the most important decisions of the assembly, even those regarding the simplest and most obvious rules of sanitation. He also criticizes them for their failure to persist in building shelters, gathering a supply of drinking water each day, and keeping up the fire. He explains once again how important the signal fire is for their eventual rescue.

An additional matter to be discussed is the unspoken fear that many of the boys have. The littl'uns, particularly, are terrified by visions of beasts in the night, and their fears are spreading. Ralph tries to explore their fears rationally in the hope of allaying them, and he is joined in this by Piggy. Jack, however, makes a speech in which he exploits the fear of beasts, and destroys Ralph's chance of success. As darkness falls, more and more of the boys grow openly frightened. Several of them tell of monsters they have heard of, like the giant squid, and discuss the possibilities of beasts and ghosts roaming the island. Fear spreads through the group.

Ralph observes all this and is powerless to control the situation. He sees that what sanity is left among them is rapidly disappearing. Nothing has been settled; the fear of beasts is only growing more serious and the boys will not agree about the importance of a signal fire. Simon attempts to explain that if there is a beast to fear, it exists within their own hearts, but the boys laugh at him. The meeting grows disorderly and chaotic. The boys scream and laugh. Jack continues to bully Piggy. Ralph attempts to regain control of the group, but is unable to do so. Jack refuses to abide by any rules except those he chooses. The boys run off, led by Jack. Only Ralph and Piggy are left.

Piggy advises Ralph to blow the conch and call the boys back to the meeting. Ralph does not do this, however, fearing that if the boys refuse to obey the summons all order will be destroyed forever. He is depressed by the lack of success that his recent effort has had and considers resigning the chieftainship, but Piggy and Simon reassure him of the need for him to retain authority. As the three boys watch, the hunters and other children complete their primitive dance and chanting and go to their huts for the night. In the darkness the only sound is that of a littl'un crying.

Commentary

For Ralph, the island is no longer a storybook kingdom. The dirt on his clothes and body distress him. His analysis of the ills of the boys is systematic and businesslike. But the nighttime meeting that begins as an attempt to reorganize the lives of the boys creates further chaos. Not only are the boys totally disorganized and more fearful than before, but they seek to forget their fears in savage behavior. The leadership of Ralph, which he sought to strengthen, has deteriorated. At the beginning, the scene on the platform had some semblance of order. Log benches had been carefully arranged before the chief's place. Ralph was careful to deliver his speech in ABC order. But he cannot handle the fearful boys. His faith in the democratic process reaches ludicrous heights as he relies on a majority vote to decide on the authenticity of ghosts. This is the climax of a series of futile attempts to legislate against fear.

If he has learned anything from his experience, he should know that no law can control the turmoil of the human imagination. By the end of the meeting, the boys are a howling mob of savages.

In this chapter, the darkness of night becomes a symbol of the confused and irrational impulses of the boys. When Piggy and Simon say that the object to fear is inside man, they approach the insight expressed by Joseph Conrad in *Heart of Darkness,* that a darkness existing in man can destroy him if not checked by imagination and reason. Conrad, too, used the jungle setting to represent the dark side of human nature, the mysterious depths of unreason and immorality. This, like Conrad's novel, is a tale of the discovery of the evil powers that lurk beneath the surface of civilized behavior.

CHAPTER 6

Beast From Air

Summary

That night, while the boys are asleep, there is a battle between aircraft in the upper atmosphere above the island. Bright lights and explosions are visible, and a parachutist floats slowly down to the island, but none of the boys see any of this. Even the twins, Sam and Eric, who are assigned to watch the signal fire through the night, have fallen asleep.

When the firewatchers awaken, they are frightened by the noise and shadows made by the parachute of the dead pilot flapping in the wind, for he has come to earth on the hilltop near them. They flee in terror to the beach below, arousing the others and giving an exaggerated account of the beast who they claim has attacked them.

Even Ralph is a bit frightened by their terrible story. After a bitter debate, an expedition of boys armed with wooden spears is organized to search the island for beasts. Many of the boys are frightened, but they are even more afraid to stay behind so everyone agrees to go. The littl'uns are left near the huts under the care of Piggy.

Eventually, the boys reach some caves on the other side of the island where no one has ever been before. Everyone is afraid, including Ralph, but he resolutely decides to search the grottoes anyway. He enters alone, since no one will accompany him, and soon discovers that he is not really frightened and does not really believe in any beasts. Soon he is joined by Jack and together the boys explore the caves and the hill above them. For a short time they again feel the comradeship and rapport that had once existed between them.

The other boys join Ralph and Jack and excitedly explore the new hill. They amuse themselves by pushing rocks into the sea and many, including Jack, are so pleased by their new discovery that they forget the purpose of the expedition. They plan to build a fort on the hill and give themselves up to games of various sorts.

Ralph becomes angry at the group and reminds them of the need for continuing to search the island, in order to allay their fears. Furthermore, they must return to the mountain that has been abandoned by Sam and Eric in order to rebuild the signal fire. The boys are uneager to do this and mutter mutinously, but they finally obey his orders and continue the march.

Commentary

The power struggle between Ralph and Jack intensifies. Clearly, as the boys move closer to primitive existence and as they recognize the island as their permanent home, Jack emerges as a powerful leader. As long as they see themselves as part of the civilized world, with rescue their main objective, Ralph, the sensible one, holds the key to the future.

The likeliest place to hunt the beast is on the mountain where he was sighted. The expedition to the rocky tip of the island seems to be a concession to the fear of the boys, who would prefer to let the signal fire go out rather than to encounter the beast on the mountain. They like the adventure of hunting, but they would prefer to hunt in the relative safety of Castle Rock. And, as the boys avoid the terrors of the jungle, so they refuse to look within themselves for fear of discovering a strange beast.

The dead pilot becomes a representation of the boys' subjective terror. The pilot's lines are tangled in rock in such a way that his body bobs back and forth. Animation is thus given to the dead form. As Sam and Eric look at the intruder, they see a strange beast, with teeth, claws and the ability to slink through the trees in pursuit. The grinning death mask, the gloves and the swinging motion of the pilot are translated, under the influence of fear, into the features and movement of a mysterious creature of destruction. The incident bears out the statements of Piggy and Simon that fear is a human product. The beast is definitely a man, and a most unformidable one — a dead man. The incident also serves as another reminder that the boys on the island are going through their conflicts against a background of war and terror in the larger world. It is ironic that the same emotions of fear and hate should predominate in both, seemingly independent, worlds.

Castle Rock represents the increased primitivism of the boys. It would be an ideal home for barbarians — a natural fortress, with caves to live in and boulders to drop on an enemy below. It invites a way of life far more primitive than that organized by Ralph on the beach. That it should be attractive to the boys indicates their readiness to accept Jack as chief, and live the life of the rock-throwing savage. When a group of boys free a boulder and send it crashing into the sea, we are reminded of the rock that Jack, Simon and Ralph pushed from the mountain in Chapter 1. These instances of the use of rock as a destructive force are a foreshadowing of the murder of Piggy in Chapter 11.

CHAPTER 7
Shadows and Tall Trees

Summary
The boys continue their hike along the shore of the island toward the hill top. While the group stops to eat, Ralph stands by himself and stares at the seemingly endless ocean surrounding the island and preventing their return to civilization. He is in the midst of a reverie composed of memories of home and fear of the unknown when he is joined by Simon. This other boy seems to be the only member of the group, aside from Piggy, who understands the gravity of their problem. He assures Ralph that somehow they will eventually be rescued. His confidence strengthens Ralph and the two boys stand together smiling.

Later in the day Jack suggests that they attempt to hunt another pig. Everyone agrees, and soon the group is in hot pursuit of a wild boar. In the melee that follows, the beast scatters them and manages to escape, giving Jack a slight wound with its tusks. Ralph has now participated in a hunt for the first time, and he suddenly begins to understand the exhilaration that the other boys feel when they are hunting and near death. Although the pig has gotten away, the boys are in a state of excitement. They re-enact the hunt in a savage dance. Robert pretends to be the pig and the others attack him. They are overcome by a frenzied bloodlust and nearly kill the boy before they self-consciously regain control of themselves.

Darkness is beginning to fall and Ralph suggests that they postpone the search of the hilltop until morning. After all, he says, if there is a beast it will do no good to attack him at night and, if there is none, as he suspects, this can only be proved in the daylight. Jack accuses him of cowardice and, finally, in order to save face, Ralph is forced to agree to climb the hill at night. Nonetheless, he insists, it is a silly idea and will do no good. Someone must go to let Piggy and the littl'uns know that the boys will not return until very late, but everyone is afraid to cross the island alone in the darkness. To the group's surprise, Simon volunteers to carry the message and immediately sets out through the jungle.

When they reach the hill, the boys mill about its base. Ralph again tries to postpone the climb, but Jack repeats his accusation, and starts up by himself. Ralph joins him and the two are followed by Roger. The remainder of the boys cluster together fearfully at the bottom.

Ralph and Roger wait halfway up the hillside while Jack climbs to the top alone. Soon he scuttles down and whispers that he has seen the beast from a distance. Ralph and Roger investigate and discover to their horror that there is indeed a strange, bulging creature in the shadows at the top. They can only make out its outlines in the darkness, but they can hear the weird flapping noise that it makes. The three terrified boys run down the hill in a panic to warn the others.

Commentary

The instinct to hunt and destroy a living creature is universal. Ralph has previously failed to recognize this instinct in himself, but now he is driven to behave like a savage. As the behavior of the boys becomes more primitive, the ritual itself

27

increases in significance, with the boys adding a drum and a pretended human victim.

There is a similar lesson concerning the dark side of man in the encounter with the grotesquely twisted corpse on the mountain. The pilot represents the deterioration of human hope. Once, he careened across the sky in a plane that represented the apex of human ingenuity and technology. But now, he has become less than a man — a mere apelike form. Because his society has used technological discoveries not for the benefit of mankind, but for destructive purposes, like the development of killer airplanes, the individual is turned into a hunter and killer of other men. Ultimately, he is reduced to a subhuman, apelike condition. The boys, who aspire so highly, with their signal fire a symbol of reason and technology, easily sink to the depths as they become hunters and live, like apes, by instinct instead of by ennobling reason. The boys could see in the apelike man on the mountain their own images now that all — even Ralph — have succumbed to the pleasures of the hunt. But they fail to read any such lesson.

If Simon were present on this journey, as he was on the first ascent, he would probably solve the mystery of the beast. Unfortunately, he has been replaced by Roger who, by his cruel treatment of the littl'uns, has identified himself as an instrument of destruction. That it is Roger, and not one of Ralph's followers, who makes the journey indicates the shift in power to the hunters that is taking place.

CHAPTER 8
Gift For the Darkness

Summary

The next morning, as news of the beast spreads among them, the boys' terror grows greater. Even Ralph is frightened and, Piggy, who was not on the hilltop, is deeply confused. Without warning, Jack grabs the conch and blows the signal for an assembly.

At the meeting, Jack announces that the existence of the beast has been definitely verified, that Ralph has questioned the skill and courage of the hunters, and that Ralph is a coward and unfit to be chief. All Ralph does, he says, is talk and give orders. He demands that the boys vote Ralph out of office.

None of the youngsters support Jack's motion. He is enraged and mortified by this. Jack angrily states that he is leaving the group and will form his own tribe, devoted to hunting and having fun, on the other side of the island. Everyone is invited to join him. Then Jack walks off alone up the beach while Ralph watches in dismay.

After he leaves, the boys show great bewilderment. Piggy, however, is overjoyed that Jack has left them and expresses his pleasure. Simon suggests that the only course remaining open is to go up the mountain again and seek the beast, but the boys are unwilling to do this and scoff at his idea. Ralph is flustered and upset by these happenings and is unable to lead the meeting or do anything constructive. He even begins to give up hope of their eventual rescue. When Piggy suggests that a new signal fire be built, on the beach instead of the mountain, Ralph realizes that they will have a chance and regains control of himself.

Before long, a new fire has been built but, when the work is finished, it is discovered that most of the boys have slipped away, evidently to join Jack. Ralph is concerned about the desertion, but Piggy tries to convince him that it is not a serious matter, and that they are better off without the others.

At the same time, Jack and his new tribe have gathered on the other side of the island and have covered their faces and bodies with barbaric war paint. They plan to build a new camp in the area called Castle Rock. The tribe sets out to hunt a pig and is successful this time. The boys derive sadistic pleasure from their cruel and bloody slaughter of the animal. The head of the dead pig is mounted on a pole and left standing in the jungle as a gift for the beast.

Piggy and Ralph sit on the beach discussing the new developments. They try to understand what has caused this break-up of their group and the inability of the boys to organize for their own survival, but are unable to discover any reason for all this. Suddenly, a party of screaming, painted boys swoops down on them, terrifying the littl'uns who are clustered in the area. The few older boys in the camp prepare to defend themselves, but the purpose of the raid is disclosed when the savages steal burning sticks from the signal fire. Before they leave, Jack announces to the remaining boys in the camp that he is chief of the new tribe and that they have established their own camp on Castle Rock. A feast is being held that night and everyone is invited. Furthermore, he may allow them to join his tribe if they behave properly.

Meanwhile, Simon has been sitting alone in the jungle, staring as if fixated at the fly-covered head of the dead pig. The heat is intense and the air is very humid and close, for a tropical storm is brewing. Suddenly, it seems as if the head — the Lord of the Flies — is speaking to him. It warns Simon that it is impossible to escape him, the beast, for he is a part of everyone, and he is responsible for all their difficulties. He threatens Simon repeatedly and finally the poor boy faints.

Commentary

The movement from order to chaos is constantly repeated. The meeting degenerates into a confusion of criticism, bragging and boasting — a covering for the fear and guilt of the boys. The fire that they enthusiastically begin to build on the beach is too large to sustain, so most of the boys simply abandon their responsibility. At the end of the chapter, most of the boys have become part of Jack's tribe of hunters. Among those who remain faithful to Ralph, there is a constant yearning for the fun and feasting of the savages that promises a further dissolution. "What makes things break up like they do?" asks Ralph. Piggy blames it on Jack. But a better answer could be found in the evil that exists not only in Jack, but in all of the boys in their tendency to destructiveness.

Wherever the author describes Simon's forest cell, he mentions butterflies that dance in the air. Because of its symmetry and delicate beauty, the butterfly has been a traditional representation of airy perfection. Simon is here worshipping the perfect form represented by the butterfly. We are not told whether this perfect form is a completely human ideal, a product of Simon's imagination, or whether it has a divine source. This question Golding wants to leave open.

The attack on the sow is more violent and shocking than the previous slaying of a pig. The boys show remarkable brutality in choosing for destruction the sow with piglets at her dugs — a picture of motherhood and domesticity. The sexual language used to describe the attack, e.g., "The sow collapsed under them and they were heavy and fulfilled upon her," suggests that the boys are fulfilling a primitive unconscious urge to violate their mothers. The killing of the sow is the climax of the book, the point at which the powers of destruction, embodied by Jack, triumph over the restraints of civilization represented by Ralph. Here, the boys totally and irrevocably commit themselves to a savage way of life.

As violent as the description of the killing of the sow appears to be, it should be noticed that Golding controls and checks the imagination of his reader. Instead of following the scene from the point of view of the boys, as he does at the beginning of the episode, he backs away and observes the event with detachment. Just before the sow is struck down, he shifts the lens of his camera from close-up to distance, taking in details of the landscape that the eyes of the boys do not observe: "She staggered into an open space where bright flowers grew and butterflies still danced, preoccupied in the centre of the clearing." The butterflies, as a contrast to the violence and brutality, symbolize the quest for pure form that the boys have now completely abandoned, as formlessness and disorder reign uninhibited. The author gives the reader the prerogative of viewing the scene of bloodlust and violence with rational detachment.

The head of the sow, hung on a stick as a gift for the beast, becomes another symbol of terror. Golding gives to the head the title "Lord of the Flies," which is a literal translation of the word *Beelzebub*, the name of a devil in the Bible. The head of the pig represents, however, not so much the evil of sin as the evil of unreason. The flies that buzz over the guts of the sow are mere instinctive beings, and they represent the primitive urges that are beginning to dominate the boys, making them as subject as flies to the influence of the Lord of the Flies. After the hunters panic and run from the head on the stick, Simon encounters it. The Lord of the Flies speaks to Simon, telling him to go away. Simon insists that the Lord of the Flies is no more than a "pig's head on a stick." The episode is a symbolic representation of the conflict between the highest and lowest impulses in man. The Lord of the Flies is explaining that there is no sense in trying to hunt and kill the beast. "You knew, didn't you? I'm part of you? Close, close, close! I'm the reason why it's no go? Why things are what they are?" The Lord of the Flies answers the question of why the civilization of the boys is a failure. The destructive element is in the boys themselves — in each boy.

Is the speech of the Lord of the Flies actually of diabolical origin, or is it a figment of Simon's imagination? It could be either. Simon is prone to fits and possesses an active imagination. At the same time, the Lord of the Flies utters truths that are beyond the knowledge of a mere boy in explaining why things are "no go" on the island. In deliberately leaving indefinite the question of the origin of the Lord of the Flies, Golding seems to be saying that it does not matter what name you give to evil, call it devil, sin, neurosis, hate, violence, brutality; the important fact is that evil exists inside man and is a necessary part of the human condition. The symbolic encounter between Simon and the Lord of the Flies represents the conflict between good and evil as it occurs in every man. And, just as Simon and the Lord of the Flies represent universal tendencies, so each of the other characters stands for a single quality — cruelty, destructiveness, creativity, or intellect — that exists to a greater or lesser degree in every man. Analyze any individual and you find in him Ralph's tendency to adventure and to common sense, Piggy's intellectualism, Simon's religious and poetic feelings, Roger's willingness to torture, Jack's appetite for destruction, Samneric's desire to please other people. How these different elements are oriented in the individual decides his moral outlook. But they are all present as impulses in the human personality. Thus, at the same time that *Lord of the Flies* is a novel exploring the disintegration of a society, it is also a study of the identity of man.

CHAPTER 9

A View to a Death

Summary

The heat and heaviness in the air increase as the storm draws near. Simon eventually revives, in a state of great exhaustion and weakness. The intensity of his emotional experience has drained him of energy and has burst the blood vessels in his nose. Determining that there is nothing else for him to do, he sets out for the mountain, barely having the strength to walk. Despite his fears and fatigue, he crawls up the hill and immediately discovers the cause of all the terror. A dead pilot lies on the hilltop, his parachute entangled in some rocks and flapping in the breeze. Simon frees the parachute lines from the impediment. Seeing the fire at Castle Rock, he staggers off to inform the other boys of what he has learned.

Piggy and Ralph decide to attend Jack's feast, partly because they are hungry and partly to attempt to keep some control over things. They are the last to arrive and find the banquet already in progress. The boys of the tribe and the others are gathered around a blazing fire and are dining on greasy roast pig and fresh fruit. Jack sits enthroned in their midst, waited upon by servants. He haughtily welcomes the two latecomers. After everyone has eaten, Jack invites those boys who have not already done so, to join his tribe. Many of them accept his offer. Ralph attempts to assert his authority as chief, but is powerless. Piggy fears that there will be a fight and urges him to leave.

As darkness begins to fall, Jack unexpectedly orders the tribe to do its dance. All the boys leap up and step wildly around the blazing fire, waving their weapons. They intone a bloodcurdling chant and grow wilder and wilder. The attraction of this savage, primeval ritual is irresistible. The hearts of the boys pound madly and they seem to lose all connection with civilization. Even Ralph and Piggy dance on the fringes of the group. Suddenly, a black shape is seen crawling from the jungle, waving and calling to them. It is Simon with his message. "The Beast!" the frenzied boys shout, "Kill the Beast!" They are somehow unable to hear or recognize their friend. The crazed boys of the tribe leap upon the helpless youngster, beating and tearing him to death, despite his cries of pain and terror.

The storm breaks in all its fury. The boys run for shelter from the torrential rains. Simon's body is washed out to sea and the body of the parachutist is blown into the lagoon by the strong winds.

Commentary

Simon's discovery of the corpse of the parachutist confirms his previous suspicion that the "beast" is an illusion prompted by the imaginations of the boys. But now that he has

33

fathomed the mysteries of the island, will he be heard and believed by the other boys? So far in the novel, the best informed boys are those least listened to.

Simon does not manage to reveal his discovery. The boys kill him and, with him, all that he represents of imaginative and religious knowledge. Because he understands the nature of evil on the island, he is a threat to the continuance of that evil, and so, that evil must destroy him. That all of the boys, including Ralph and Piggy, join in the murderous assault indicates the universality of guilt. The author wants to stress that the potential for such a horrendous crime as the murder of Simon and the destruction of imagination exists in every man.

At the same time that the boys are submitting to evil influences, they are fulfilling a natural desire to deposit all of their guilt in a scapegoat. A scapegoat (originally an actual goat sacrificed to God so that men could *escape* blame for their sins) is any man, animal, or thing to which is attributed the guilt of a group of people. The boys, feeling guilty about their past failures and crimes, try to lose fear and self-awareness in a ritual act of murder in which Simon becomes a "beast," responsible for the presence of evil on the island. Previously, the pigs were scapegoats through which the boys sought to lose feelings of guilt and inadequacy in the violent act of murder. But, as often happens in unhealthy societies, the first act only increases the need for purgation, and the killings become progressively more criminal, going from pig to sow and, finally, to a human victim who relieves, momentarily at least, the common guilt. Sir James Frazer, in *The Golden Bough*, includes an entire chapter on scapegoats, describing the scores of ways that primitive tribes ceremonially deposit their guilt on a single object, animal, or person and then proceed to harm or destroy the guilt-laden creature. Often, the primitive tribe will use sticks to beat the scapegoat, as the boys do.

The significance of the vanishing of the parachute and corpse into the sea at the moment of Simon's death is that now the beast on top of the mountain is no longer necessary. His place is to be supplied by human beasts. It is ironic that Simon, who hoped to dispel the beast by enlightening the boys, instead replaces the beast as the imagined source of evil. After

Simon, the savage society will turn its violence against Piggy, and then Ralph.

CHAPTER 10

The Shell and the Glasses

Summary

The next morning, Ralph and Piggy are ashamed and reticent when they meet each other on the beach. Both of them are bruised and dirty. They discover that everyone has joined Jack, except the twins, Sam and Eric, and a few littl'uns.

Both boys are uncertain about what to do and are unwilling to discuss freely the events of the night before. Ralph is deeply troubled by his memories, but Piggy fearfully tries to ascribe Simon's death to an accident. Besides, he says, they were only on the fringes of the dancing tribe and are not directly responsible for anything that might have happened. Ralph's conscience will not permit him to accept this easy excuse and he painfully insists that a murder has taken place and that they were both accomplices. Piggy is horrified at this idea and again repeats his rationalization. At last, Ralph helplessly and uncertainly agrees that Piggy is right. Sam and Eric appear, looking exhausted and ashamed, and they also deny having participated in the fatal dance.

At Castle Rock Jack rules his tribe harshly. One of the boys, Wilfred, is punished brutally for some minor and unrevealed infraction of his rules. Roger, a young sadist, has become his second in command, and the other boys now live in frightened obedience to their leaders. Several of them express bewilderment and guilt about the happenings at the dance. Jack convinces them that it was indeed the beast who appeared, although in disguise. Furthermore, he says, they must continue to be alert and watchful, for the beast is not really dead. No one can kill the beast and there will always be danger. In addition, they must guard their camp well, for Ralph and his followers are also dangerous; they will do anything in their power to spoil things for the tribe. The next day, Jack continues, there will be another hunt and once again they will leave the head as a gift for the beast. Tonight, he and a few others will arrange to get fire from the boys on the beach.

After sunset, the few boys remaining in the old camp retire to their hut. They have been trying to keep the signal fire alive, but are slowly becoming depressed and listless. It is hard for them to remember the purpose of the fire without mental effort, and the labor involved is too difficult for such a small group. Later on, they are awakened by eerie voices in the darkness. Then, without warning, a group of screaming boys swoops down on the hut, collapsing it. A short and violent fight follows in which the defenders cannot see their adversaries, and end up beating each other. The raiders leave as quickly as they came.

The boys examine their wounds and wonder why Jack and his tribe persist in tormenting them. They cannot understand why they were molested since they are quite willing to share the fire with the others if asked. Piggy's moans soon inform them of the enemy's purpose: they have stolen his eyeglasses so as to use the remaining lens for a burning glass.

Commentary

Although Jack and his followers pretend that their victim was an unknown beast, they are obviously so guilt-ridden after the murder of Simon that they try to drown their consciences in new violence. Without cause, Jack beats one of the boys. He has a rock poised on the cliff — a symbol of his mortal hatred for Ralph and Piggy.

The stealing of Piggy's glasses represents the complete defeat of the intellectual by the savage. Now, Ralph, who has been relying more and more on Piggy in recent chapters, has, for all practical purposes, lost his brain trust, and Jack rules as the absolute monarch of the island domain.

The sand castles of Chapter 4 have been destroyed and with them the romantic adventure and hopefulness of youth. Here, the scene is a castle of rock, a natural home for a primitive cave man. Jack and his followers have become creatures of instinct. Both civilized forms and romantic dreams have been replaced by the law of survival of the fittest. All hopes for the rescue of the group and the return to civilization are swallowed in a wave of destructive passion. Kill or be killed becomes the motto of the group of boys whose hearts have turned as hard as Castle Rock.

CHAPTER 11

Castle Rock

Summary

Ralph, Piggy and the twins sit near the ashes of their extinguished fire the next morning, bemoaning their fates and tending their injuries. Although there are only four of them, they go through the formal ritual of holding an assembly at which they discuss their predicament. It is decided that they will go to Castle Rock in order to talk with Jack, in the hope of making him see reason. Not only is there no longer a signal fire, but Piggy is nearly blind without his glasses, so they have a sense of urgency about their mission. They plan to take the conch, Ralph's symbol of authority, with them as a reminder to the tribe of the order and sanity which once prevailed on the island.

When the tiny group arrives at Castle Rock, it discovers that the entrance is guarded by armed members of the tribe. The sentries ignore Ralph's trumpet call on the conch and mock him or toss stones. They continue to taunt Ralph and his friends until Jack and a group of hunters, carrying a dead pig, emerge from the jungle behind the four boys.

The two leaders confront each other. Jack orders Ralph to return to his own side of the island. Ralph demands that Jack give back Piggy's glasses, points out the cruelty of keeping them, and accuses Jack of theft. Jack is infuriated and lunges at him, and the two boys wrestle for an instant before separating. Ralph repeats his demand and earnestly tries to make Jack understand the necessity for a signal fire. Jack responds by having his hunters disarm and bind Sam and Eric. Ralph is unable to control his fury at this unprovoked act and he shouts his denunciations at Jack. The other boy attacks him again and the two are quickly engaged in a bitter hand-to-hand fight.

They are interrupted by the pathetic cries of Piggy, who is desperately trying to make himself heard over the uproar. The tribe mocks the helpless, nearly blind boy and laughs at him as he tries to convince them of the need for justice and sensible organization. Even as he speaks, Roger pushes a huge boulder down the slope toward him. Piggy hears the noise, but cannot see the source of danger. He and the conch are both crushed beneath the great rock.

An instant later, the boys of the tribe hurl their spears at Ralph in obedience to Jack's orders, but he manages to escape into the jungle where he hides. Meanwhile, Jack and Roger torture the twins in order to force them to join the tribe.

Commentary

In Chapter 4, Roger, restrained by habits of civilized behavior, could not throw stones directly at a human being. Early in this chapter, as Roger removes his hands from the log under the boulder above the entrance to Castle Rock, in order to throw stones at the twins, Golding makes the comment that "Some source of power began to pulse in Roger's body." The power is now stronger than any habitual restraint. It is the destructive power of prehistoric man who kills his victims with primitive weapons. When Ralph shouts at Jack, "Which is better, laws, and rescue, or hunting and breaking things up?" he summarizes the conflicts in the book between the ideals of modern society and the impulses of primitive man. Roger provides an answer, first in the stones that he throws at Piggy, then in the huge boulder. He and Jack have become complete savages.

When Piggy is thrown into the sea, he lands first on a red rock, then is swept away by the retreating sea. The red rock is like an altar on which Piggy is sacrificed to the forces of destruction represented in Roger's stones and boulder, and in the motion of the all-consuming sea. The event symbolizes the obliteration of intellect and reason from the island. After the most exalted flowering of society in the ideals of religion and poetry is destroyed with the death of Simon, the intellectual forms of society, the highly developed laws of social intercourse, are killed. The experience on the island is the story of human civilization in reverse. The smashing of the conch shell at the moment of Piggy's death represents the loss of the traditional systems of authority so cherished by Piggy. It is appropriate that the sea, which Triton controlled by blowing his conch, should rear up and snatch Piggy after the conch is shattered.

CHAPTER 12

Cry of the Hunters

Summary

For the remainder of the day Ralph stays hidden in the jungle, trying to understand the strange events on the island. He is unable to comprehend how a group of civilized school-boys whom he once knew well, has now become a band of cruel and barbaric, painted savages. Eventually, he discovers the pig's head which has been left in the jungle as a gift for the beast and is astonished by it. He arms himself with the sharpened stick upon which it had been mounted.

When darkness falls, Ralph sneaks near to the tribal camp where a feast is in progress, and finds that Sam and Eric are on guard duty. The two boys are frightened by his presence and are unwilling to join forces with him. Nonetheless, they give him food and warn him that Jack plans to arm all the boys and search the entire island for him the next day. There are horrible tortures waiting if he is captured. Ralph tells them where he plans to conceal himself, hoping that they will guide the tribe away from his hiding place.

All night Ralph huddles in a nearly impenetrable thicket not far from Castle Rock, afraid to let himself fall asleep. In the morning, he hears voices nearby and learns that the twins have revealed his whereabouts. Several boys attempt to enter his refuge, but it is an easy place to defend and he manages to fight them off. Soon, however, Jack has the whole area set on fire in order to smoke him out.

Ralph is forced to leave his hiding place and manages to break through the line of his enemies. He thrashes his way through the jungle in a panic, looking wildly for a place of safety. The tribe continues to pursue him. Jack and his followers systematically comb the island, leaving an ever smaller area for Ralph to hide in. Meanwhile, the fire has spread and much of the jungle is now burning, but this does not deter the tribe from its "hunt." As his pursuers draw nearer, the already frightened Ralph becomes terrified. He instinctively thinks only of escape, like an animal, and hopelessly searches for a safe hideout.

At last Ralph is driven to the beach. There is nowhere else to go and he can hear the voices of his pursuers close behind him. Ralph collapses in exhaustion, but when he looks up he discovers a naval officer standing before him. The officer is cheerful and explains that his ship was attracted by the smoke of the burning island.

The painted savages reach the shore also. Upon seeing the officer and sailors, they stop and stare silently. The officer becomes serious when he sees the condition of the boys. He questions Ralph and is shocked and dismayed when he learns that several boys have been killed and that nearly all traces of organization and civilization have disappeared from the island. Ralph realizes that at last he is free from all the horrors of life on the island and feels secure in the knowledge that he has been rescued. As he recalls the things that have taken place, he bursts into tears. The other boys soon begin weeping also. The officer is touched and embarrassed by this sight and turns his back in order to give the boys time to compose themselves. While they cry, he contemplates the sight of his cruiser anchored in the lagoon.

Commentary

When Ralph encounters the Lord of the Flies, he goes through an experience similar to Simon's before his death. Though he knocks over the pig's skull, it keeps grinning at him, as if to remind him that it is part of him, just as it was of Simon, and just as it is of all the boys. Jack, Simon and Ralph may be very different types, but they are alike in their proneness to evil. Though Ralph and Simon try to ignore the destructive force within themselves, and Jack tries to submerge his good impulses, each boy is a battleground where the forces of corruption wage war on the forces of good. Each boy is a mixture of good and evil. When Samneric confide to Ralph that Roger has sharpened a stick at both ends to use for him, they reveal the extent of the debasement of the boys. Ralph is to be treated like the sow, his head stuck in the ground on a stick sharpened at both ends, his body cooked and eaten by the cannibalistic boys. When Ralph, himself, to avoid detection, relies on cunning like that of the pig, he reveals how easily it is for a human to slip into the role of beast.

The officer, pompous, precise, proud of his clothes and

trim cutter, suffers from the same moral blindness that Ralph did early in the book. On the other hand, wearing a gun and commanding a gun boat, he possesses a power of destruction like Jack's. He, too, in spite of his dignity and fondness for a "good show," is a hunter who fails to recognize the vileness of his career. And, though he is, like the primitive hunters on the island, obsolete in a future world of atomic warfare and supersonic air travel, he is a symbol of the chain of destruction present on the island and continuous in the "civilized" world. At the end, Ralph is crying "for the end of innocence, the darkness of man's heart, and the fall through the air of the true, wise friend called Piggy." The officer, embarrassed, turns away. This is no way for British boys to carry on. The officer's ideas about British boys are as out-of-date as his weapons. He is a throwback to the days when England was still Queen of the Seas, and when such a title had some importance.

Ralph's phrase, "the darkness of man's heart," is an allusion to Conrad's *Heart of Darkness*, where a similar concept of self-recognition is expressed. In every man, according to Conrad, there is a darkness that he must discover. Either he sees and controls this dark presence, or it dominates him. To ignore the fact of evil is to destroy all possibility of learning from it. This theme of Conrad's becomes the lesson represented in the boys' experience on the island.

At the end of the novel, the entire island is scorched by fire — another example of the irresponsibility of the boys. The island, more than ever, resembles a city consumed by atomic warfare.

Structure

1. Analysis

The simplest and, at the same time, the most important method of dealing with the question of how a novel is structured is to begin by standing back a good distance from the story and looking at its overall direction. A question one should always ask oneself is: "In what condition are the characters at the beginning of the novel, and at the end?" A second question to ask is, "How did they get that way?" The answers to these two questions constitute a description of the structure.

Structure should not be confused, however, with plot; for while these are related, they are not the same. The plot of a novel is the story it tells. The actions of the plot are explained by the circumstances the characters are in, the nature of the characters themselves and the motivations of the characters — what makes them do what they do. When one talks about plot, one explains what happens by saying that the characters were doing thus and so, or thought such and such. But when one is talking about structure, one is talking about the way the *author* makes things happen, not the characters. Thus, when a lens of Piggy's glasses is broken we may explain this by saying that Jack hates Piggy, or that he attacks Piggy because he doesn't dare attack Ralph. If we offer this explanation we are talking about the plot. On the other hand, if we say that the lens is broken because William Golding *wants it broken* as a device for showing that reason (represented by Piggy) is being slowly blinded on the island, we are talking about structure. Obviously, both kinds of comments are necessary to form a complete statement about the events of a novel.

From this point of view, we can see that the novelist has a double job to perform. He must make the things happen in his book that he wants to happen, yet he cannot offer as his reason a simple "I wanted it that way, dear reader." He must find a reason that is consistent with his characters. This means that to discuss structure it becomes necessary to look *through* the plot constantly, and ask why the author, as well as the characters, are working things out as they are. It takes a very good writer to make both his structure (why the author wants things to happen) and the plot (why the characters are the way they are) believable. To some extent, *Lord of the Flies* is a science-fiction story, since it is set in the future, a future determined by science. But we do not find the structure unbelievable, because with two world wars behind us, we know that a third is possible. Therefore, the structure itself is possible. If we also find the characters and their motivations believable, we will tend to say that the novel is a good one.

If we were to illustrate the structure of this novel, we might begin with the question, "In what condition are the characters at the beginning of the novel and at the end?" Then we would describe a world at war, out of which a number of fairly typical English boys are dropped on a pleasant South Sea island to look after themselves. At the end of the novel their condition parallels the war-torn world of adults. Their condition is nightmarish. Three are dead: one by accident, one by frenzied excitement and one by sadistic murder. Another is about to be killed and decapitated in a cruelly inhuman way. Most of the boys have entirely lost their identities as nice, well-brought-up English lads, and have reverted entirely to mindless savagery. One of them cannot even remember his name. The next question, "How did they get this way?" is answered by tracing out the steps by which this degeneration has taken place.

This approach to analyzing structure can then be applied to each chapter. For the overall changes that the novel records are subdivided into lesser changes that occur along the way. By asking oneself, "In what condition are the characters at the beginning and end of this chapter," one can get at the structure of the chapter. Then, answering the question, "How did they get this way," will supply the motives. But, again, it should be remembered that when the answer given is in terms of motivation of the characters, one is talking about plot, one aspect of structure. When the answer given explains the author's purpose, one is discussing the structure itself.

2. Form

The formal approach to structure is based on the assumption that the author only puts into his novel events which are actually necessary in some way to achieve the total effect he is seeking. In other words, all of the chapters and paragraphs, all of the incidents and characters, everything in the book is there because it is a necessary part. Nothing is left out but nothing is added, either. Most good novelists write this way, and many have discussed in essays and articles precisely the point that there should not be anything in a novel which is not strictly necessary. Writing which follows this guideline is called "organic." That is, every part of the organic novel is taken to be essential in some way to every other part, and every part is taken to be connected with the whole. To say that a novel is organic, as Henry James, the American novelist, has observed, is to say that it is a living thing, like a human body with its arms and legs — parts that go to make up the total person — and that all of the novel's parts go into giving it an artistic "life." Criticism which undertakes to explain a novel by showing how all its parts relate to the overall plan, is called "organic criticism."

3. Organic Unity

The term "organic unity" can be used in reference to a novel's success in interrelating all the chapters, events, the motivation of the characters, the hidden purposes of the author, in a word, everything. *Lord of the Flies* has organic unity in a high degree because it is possible to show at any point in the novel, even in apparently trivial details, that the author is constantly working toward his goal, and never allows himself to wander from his purposes. The slight scene in Chapter 4, showing the littl'un, Henry, at play on the beach is handled to stress Henry's illusion of power over nature, a theme that ties in with the fire that sweeps the island at the end and with Golding's view that science, which attempts to control and harness nature, is a very dangerous plaything when it is used in waging war. So, even here, a trifling activity is described in terms of the total work of art. A good critic should be able to make such comments about any incident in the book.

4. Esthetic Unity

Another aspect of organic form, one that is quite easy to see but hard to talk about, is esthetic unity. One of the ways a writer achieves his purposes is by creating an emotional atmosphere, a mood. If he wants his readers to feel apprehensive that all is not going well with his characters, he may describe rather gloomy, shadowy scenes. All during the afternoon when Simon talks with the Lord of the Flies and climbs the mountain to see the "beast," we hear the rumble of thunder and see that it is clouding up. The weather and the approaching darkness are made to connect with the disaster that is in the making. Notice that Golding often ends a chapter with a certain mood, then uses the same mood to start the next one. This device also contributes to esthetic unity. Thus, Chapter 3 ends with Simon squatting in the forest retreat he has found. The "riotous colors" of the day have all faded. And Chapter 4 begins with a description of the morning colors as being "pearl" and "opalescence," again very bland colors.

5. Setting

Related to a consideration of esthetic unity is the appropriateness of the physical setting used. In *Lord of the Flies*, Golding has apparently worked out a series of setting contrasts, designed to coincide with the actions and mood he is portraying. Opposed are the lagoon versus the open sea, the mountain versus Castle Rock, the beach versus the jungle and night versus day. Golding shows the lagoon as a safe, dreamy place of mirages where the water is warmer than body temperature. There, Ralph can dream of rescue, or play "suppose." In contrast, Golding uses the open sea on the other side of the island as the setting for a hard kind of reality where no dreams are possible. The water is cold there, and the island unprotected by any coral reef. He uses the mountain as the high place, where truth can be seen (that they are on an island, that the "beast" is a dead man), idealism and hope (the fire, hope of rescue). In contrast to the mountain, he uses Castle Rock, way at the other end of the island, as a jumbled, mix-up of rocks with a cave in the center, to accord with the regression of the boys to savagery and primitive superstition (they guard the gate against the "beast"). The beach, a familiar, easy-going place, where Ralph prefers to stay, is contrasted with the wilder jungle, to which Jack is drawn by his compulsion to hunt, and Simon is drawn by his desire to be alone in a surrounding of peace and beauty. Golding contrasts daylight settings, which he connects with Ralph and Piggy and "reason," to night settings, the time of mystery and dread, which seems to suit Jack and, again, the mysterious Simon.

6. Symbolism

Most often, a symbol in a novel is based upon an image. An image is something that can be recognized by one or more of the five senses; it can be seen, heard, tasted, felt or smelled. The image is then made to stand in place of an abstraction which cannot be easily visualized: an idea, or perhaps an ideal. Symbols can be divided into two large categories, both of which appear in *Lord of the Flies*: public symbols and private symbols. A public symbol is one which anyone can understand without explanation, since it uses images that are familiar to everyone. A private symbol is one which must be explained by the author, since its meaning is arbitrarily assigned by him. Thus, when we see the crosses on the choir boys' cloaks, we know without further explanation that they are Christians, and that they are supposed to think and behave like Christians (follow the Golden Rule, the Ten Commandments, and so on). Daytime and darkness are also symbols which are self-explanatory. This is also true of the mountain as a high place, or the lagoon as a safe place. These are public symbols because they have fairly universal meanings. But the novel also makes use of private symbols which do not mean the same things in the world at large as they mean in a book. What is the meaning, for example, of a pair of glasses? All they mean is that the wearer has some defect of vision which the glasses help to correct. But Golding has made Piggy's glasses into a private symbol. For the purposes of his novel, he has arbitrarily indicated that the glasses will have something to do with reason. That way, the loss of one lens, then the weakening of Piggy's eyes and, finally, the theft of the glasses can be used to show the progressive loss of reasonable behavior among the boys. Or what does a conch shell mean in the world? It is something interesting to look at, pretty, maybe, but that is about all. But Golding has made a private symbol of the conch by turning it into the emblem of Ralph's rule. It symbolizes Ralph's power. We could also show that a stick pointed at both ends is a private symbol, defined only by its use in this particular novel, or a dead airman, or a pig's head on a stick. These are all private symbols the author has given special meanings to. Outside of the novel, they do not mean the same things at all. Scholars also are able to recognize a third kind of symbolism which need not concern us here, called "unconscious symbolism." This is symbolism which the writer has created without realizing it, out of his own unconscious fears and loves.

Chart: Guide by Chapter to Main Action and Location

(1. Platform, Mountain) Ralph assembles the boys by blowing the conch; he is elected leader. Ralph, Jack and Simon climb the mountain.	(2. Platform, Mountain) The boys discuss plans, fears, then climb mountain and light a fire. The fire burns out of control and kills a littl'un.	(3. Jungle, Beach, Jungle) Jack hunts; Ralph builds shelters. Simon goes off by himself to a hiding place in the jungle.	(4. Beach, Mountain) Jack kills a pig, but lets fire go out. A lens of Piggy's glasses is broken.
(5. Platform) Ralph lectures the boys on following the rules. "Things are breaking up." Jack breaks up the meeting.	(6. Mountain, Platform, Castle Rock) A dead airman is parachuted down. Samneric mistake him for a beast. Ralph takes a search party to Castle Rock looking for the beast.	(7. Jungle, Mountain) A boar charges into the boys and escapes. Ralph, Jack and Roger climb the mountain and see the "beast." They flee in terror.	(8. Beach, Jungle, Beach) Jack splits with Ralph, taking his hunters. He kills a sow. Simon talks with the Lord of the Flies. Ralph lights a fire on the beach.
(9. Mountain, Beach) Simon solves the mystery of the beast. Jack gives a feast. The boys dance and kill Simon when he stumbles into their circle.	(10. Beach, Castle Rock, Beach) Ralph, Piggy and Samneric try to keep fire going. Jack's tribe has moved into Castle Rock. Jack steals Piggy's glasses.	(11. Beach, Castle Rock) Ralph, Piggy and Samneric go to Castle Rock to demand return of Piggy's glasses. Piggy is killed, Samneric are captured. Ralph is driven away.	(12. Jungle, Castle Rock, Jungle, Beach) Ralph is hunted down by Jack's party, who set island on fire. A ship sees the smoke and rescues the boys.

Questions and Answers on Structure

Question 1.
Describe Jack's connection with the structure of the novel.

Answer
The novel's entire structure is determined by the presence of Jack. Ralph, the protagonist, is a passive hero. He is not a hero who acts upon others, unlike the heroes of many novels, but one who is acted upon by others. If he had his way, the boys would live quietly, eating fruit and swimming, and taking turns maintaining a fire until a ship came to rescue them. Jack is the antagonist, whose role is to provide a foil for the hero. He sets up the tensions of the novel and permits the author to show us his purposes. It is Jack who breaks up the first meeting by running off to build a fire on the mountain. Jack also provides the tension between future hopes and present pleasures. Ralph is content to starve along on fruit, living for his hope of rescue. Jack, on the other hand, wants his enjoyment *now*, not in some distant, hazy future. He would rather eat meat, and spend his time hunting, than see that the signal fire is never allowed to go out. Jack is also responsible for the main sociological event of the novel, the splitting up of the boys into two parties, one peaceable and the other warlike. His influence upon the structure is one of almost complete domination from start to finish. As the society shapes up in its final form, all the boys are allied with Jack, the new chief, with the exception of Ralph, who is now an outcast from the established society.

Question 2.
Is *Lord of the Flies* structured so as to present equally balanced forces?

Answer
Not at all. Since Golding defines force as primarily social, the physical strength of an individual does not count. Ralph is the biggest boy, physically, and probably is the strongest. But his size and strength are no help to him at all. If the contest of leadership could be decided by a fistfight, a different story

might be told, but not a true one. For Golding intends a parallel between the adventures of the boys and the realities of the world. Since Golding sees the world as a savage place, and mankind as essentially primitive under its veneer of civilization, he must show Jack emerging as the representative of superior force. This, Jack accomplishes through his ability to manipulate other boys. True, he is strong enough to kill a wild pig, but he needs a circle of other boys to trap the pig first. Jack is seen from the start as a leader and manipulator, when we see him marching his choir down the beach. This talent is what enables him to break up the first meeting; when he calls out "Follow me," all the boys do. It enables him to order his hunters to follow him on a hunt. And it enables him to win all the big'uns (using force when necessary) away from "the conch." One showdown in the power struggle occurred when Jack managed to get the boys to stay at his feast and do their dance in answer to their fear of the coming storm, instead of hiding in the shelters as Ralph wanted them to do. This maneuver resulted in Simon's death, for obviously, if the boys had followed Ralph, they would have gone to the shelters and Simon would have lived to explain the mystery of the beast, and so end all their fears. The reason the world keeps having bigger and deadlier wars is that people like Jack, rather than Ralph, manage to get into positions of power. That is why Ralph's struggle is downhill all the way. The novel starts with the dream of an ideal society, but it ends with the nightmare of real life.

Question 3.

How does Golding achieve a tonal unity?

Answer

Two main devices are used to achieve tonal unity among the parts of *Lord of the Flies*. One is through the thematic use of fear, and the other is through the tension developed between logical, common sense plans, and illogical, momentary impulses.

Chapter 1 establishes a gay mood, considering that the boys are stranded on an uninhabited island. It looks as though they are going to have a lot of fun. But by the end of the chapter, Jack is slamming his knife into a tree and promising himself that "next time" he will kill a pig. Implied violence is seen here, a cause for some concern. In Chapter 2, the littl'uns reveal their fears of a "beastie," which the older ones laugh at, but can't quite get rid of. And, throughout the rest of the novel, violence and fear ride hand in hand over the terrified boys. All of their activities, even those as tame as going swimming in the lagoon, are set against their fears and the violence with which they answer these. The reader knows that the fears are of imaginary things, but the boys do not. And whether the cause is imaginary or real, the fear itself is real, and so are the actions arising from it. The actions of the boys are sometimes logical and sometimes illogical. Yet these actions do not in any way break down the structural unity of the story. When Ralph makes a logical proposal that the boys maintain a signal fire, enthusiasm and emotion take over. The boys rush out and thoughtlessly create a huge and dangerous bonfire. There is no loss of unity here, for the boys are acting very much the way young boys act when carried away by enthusiasm. Ralph makes sensible rules about keeping fresh water on hand and using the rocks for a lavatory. But the littl'uns continue to defecate in the same place where they pick their fruit and, of course, keeping drinking water handy turns out to be a bother and is gradually forgotten. Tension is created between the logical and sensible, on the one hand, and lack of organization and boredom with routine on the other. We find that the characters are often illogical and inconsistent, but they are only so in ways that are entirely familiar to us. Since fear is the pervading emotion which directs the boys' behavior, all of their inconsistencies are easily and believably motivated by keying them to that fear.

Question 4.

How do the conflicts presented connect with the structure?

Answer

Psychological tension between opposing forces provides the cement for holding the various parts of the novel together. From the start of the story, Jack is shown to be a natural leader, yet Ralph is elected to head the boys, by an overwhelming majority. We are aware from the start that a possible rivalry could follow. As the story progresses, this rivalry becomes increasingly intense. At length, Jack will taunt Ralph with the charge that he is a coward, and Ralph will reply with a sensible admission that if a monster is dwelling on the mountaintop, he ought to be afraid. But Ralph will finally be swayed into making a wrong judgment, because of the intensity of the rivalry. His mistake of seeing the dead airman in the dark will result in Simon's death, as well as his own loss of control over the boys and, finally, his loss of leadership. In deciding to climb the mountain in the dark, Ralph is under the psychological tension of his rivalry with Jack, but he is also under an inner tension within himself. He must decide whether he can do what he knows is best, even when others tell him he is being a coward, or whether he must trust the judgment of others over his own. This last is what Ralph chooses to do, and his choice results in failure. We see that he is not sure of himself; that he is the victim of inner tension.

These conflicts are united in the same way light and darkness are united in a single day. Just as a day has both light and dark, so the psychological tensions exist only because of their opposites. We would not have any idea of night if there were only daytime. And, similarly, any decision or action of the novel is defined by its opposite. The rationality of keeping a smoky fire going is juxtaposed against the irrationality of hunting pigs and letting the fire go out. The easygoing leadership of Ralph is set against the disciplined choir (then hunters). When we see Ralph dreaming on the shore, we remember Jack sniffing the ground deep in the jungle, for traces of pig droppings. When we see the hunters in their savage dance, we contrast that with Ralph diving into the lagoon, or splashing water on Piggy. When we are shown what "should be" (the ideal society), it is contrasted with what "is" (the degenerating society); and, finally, at the end, we weep with Ralph for the contrast between what "is," and what "might have been."

Characterization

1. Description

Every known factor about a given character must be taken into consideration when describing him. In the actual description, however, the principle of selection will have to be used, since it is not usually possible to include all of the details. In a highly organic novel like *Lord of the Flies*, we have already seen that every detail is there for a reason. Since a character description must be limited to the essential points, it becomes necessary to decide which traits are necessary to mention for a particular kind of description. If a character is being described in connection with his role as a "type," the traits that connect him with his type will have to be mentioned. If he is being considered as an individual, those aspects of character, which seem to set him apart as different from others, become important. If his symbolic role is being stressed, the description should dwell upon whatever qualifies him as a symbol. Thus, if one were to describe Ralph as a "type" of the British middle class, it would be necessary to talk about his family background, what his father does for a living, what kind of home Ralph comes from. On the other hand, if one were to describe Ralph as an individual, his more personal qualities, such as his sense of responsibility, his tendency to dream, would be given a great deal more attention than his family background. If one were to discuss Ralph as a symbol, the selection of details would be still different. Here, such characteristics as his yellow hair, his being the tallest boy, his quietness, and later on, his appearance with dead leaves in his hair, all might appropriately be mentioned. As can be seen, these three approaches to a description of character result in the selection of different details or, in some cases, make different use of the same details. Consider what would happen if one tried to crowd in all of the details mentioned in connection with any one character. In order to make any sense at all of the details, it would be necessary to enter into perhaps three or more discussions at one time. The description would be a mass of digressions and inconsistencies. If a student is called upon to present a complete description, he would do well to break down the character's appearance and traits into

53

groupings, and discuss the meaning of these different groupings separately. This will avoid getting into the kind of hopeless incoherence that results from trying to do more than one thing at a time.

2. Character Development or Revelation

Any novel has characters, and since the novelist has a story to tell, his characters undergo changes of situation. These changes are reflected in turn within a given character in one of two ways: the character may be shown to change, to "develop" as the story progresses, or he may simply be more fully revealed to us, but still remain essentially the same as he was at the start. When a character undergoes fundamental changes, we speak of character development. When he does not change, but is simply defined more fully — revealed — by the events of the story, we speak of character revelation. Here, we enter upon one of the most difficult problems in analyzing literature. All one has to go on is his judgment, and a single error can result in a false conclusion. The best method is to ask oneself a series of questions and try to establish answers. Let us try this method with Roger, to illustrate how such an analysis might be managed. The questions and answers are of course by the student to himself.

Q. Is Roger a developing character or a character who is simply more fully revealed as the story progresses?
A. How should I know?
Q. How would you describe his character at the end of the novel?
A. He's a murderer. He likes to torture little kids. All of the boys except Jack seem to be afraid of him.
Q. But what about his behavior earlier in the story? Do you see him doing things to hurt, along the way?
A. Well, he does throw stones in a circle around Henry, and we are told that he would throw to hit, except that he still remembers from his old life that he was told not to throw stones. Yet, I guess he wants to hurt Henry, all right; it's just that he doesn't dare, yet.
Q. Anything else?

A. Well, that business about shoving the pointed stick into the pig was cruel. Now that I think of it, he was planning something like that for Ralph.

Q. So he's really the same person all along, isn't he: at first, he wants to hurt but doesn't dare. Now, what about the very beginning? Is he a nice little boy when he first is seen in the story — are you missing something there?

A. I don't think so, because he is first described as being very sullen. He doesn't act as if he even wants to tell his name.

Q. Then would you say that Roger is a developing character or a revealed character?

A. He's a revealed character. He never changes, it's just that as the story moves along we get to know him better as he has opportunities to do the kinds of things he wanted to do all along.

Character analysis does not come easy. But if this method of asking and answering questions is used, the reasons begin to stand out clearly for the different characters, and a great deal can be learned.

3. Motivation

Closely connected with most character analysis is the question: *Why* does the character do, or say, or think as he does? Here, one is dealing with the psychological aspects of character. Sometimes, the author tells us what his character is thinking, or why he did this or that. At other times, he leaves hints along the way. And, occasionally, the author presents totally unmotivated acts. The reader must decide whether the motivation is hidden in the character and can be discovered, or whether no clues at all are available. In *Lord of the Flies,* motivation is carefully handled. Even the senseless cruelty of Roger can be explained to a degree; he is getting his kicks by hurting — he may be deriving a perverted sexual satisfaction from torture. Even the idle play of Henry on the beach is motivated. Henry is imagining that he has power over the little sea creatures, while the incoming tide is making him move back — is using its superior force over him. And Piggy's bright mind is motivated — it doesn't just happen that he is bright.

We learn that he has spent a lot of time sick in bed, when he could do nothing at all but think. Gradually, he acquired skill through practice. It is seldom safe to assume that a character is behaving in a totally unmotivated fashion. When such a situation appears, it probably means that the reader has not looked carefully at the evidence.

Character Delineation Chart

	RALPH	JACK	PIGGY	SIMON	ROGER	SAMNERIC
Character "Type"	model boy	ruthless leader	thinker	mystic	sadist	followers
Central Motivation	to be rescued	to hunt	to be rescued	to know the truth	to hurt	to help
Principal Actions	forms democracy; lights signal fire	splits boys into two groups; hunts down Ralph	"feeds" ideas to Ralph	talks to Lord of the Flies; solves mystery of the beast	kills Piggy	first to see the "beast"
Principal Emotions and Attributes	dreamer; easy-going, but very responsible	hatred; a natural leader	serious; thoughtful	visionary; brave	quiet; a "loner"	have no separate identities
at the beginning of the novel	happy; excited by adventure	in charge of a boys' choir	apprehensive; frightened	fainting; choir-boy	small, dark boy	carefree twins
at the end of the novel	hunted like an animal	the chief of a band of savages	murdered	murdered	a savage	savages

Character Sketches

Ralph

He is a tall, good-looking boy with blond hair. He comes from a "good" English family. His father is a naval officer of some rank, and he remembers a pleasant home life of seacoast cottages, "treats" before bed, books to read and a walled garden visited by wild ponies. He is a representative of the genteel, British middle class. He is a dreamer, rather than an active doer of deeds. At home, he liked to lie down in a shed and watch the snowflakes falling. On the island, he goes to sleep by allowing himself to make up fantasies, games of "suppose," in which he imagines himself back home and reunited with his family. Ralph is a likeable boy, although he is not a very good thinker. He seldom sees the significance of things until someone points it out to him. When pressed to make a decision, he seems unequipped to think out the problem, and as often as not he makes the wrong choice. Ralph's calling a meeting at twilight to talk about fear with the littl'uns was one of his worst misjudgments. It permitted Jack to defy him, and break up the meeting. After this loss of control, Ralph was never able to maintain his position with security. At the end of the story, Ralph is shown to have learned a great and bitter lesson: his dream world, and his idealism have been crushed. He is a disillusioned realist who now sees the world and its people for what they are.

Jack

He is tall and thin, a little smaller than Ralph, red-haired and ugly. He is British, as are all the boys, but nothing is known of his background. Claire Rosenfield, a noted critic, regards Jack as a Satan figure, an explanation that seems to account for his red hair. Jack is already something of a world traveller at the start of the novel. He mentions having been at Gibraltar and Addis Ababa with his choir. He handles his choir with firm discipline and extracts obedience. While the boys are giving their first names to Piggy, Jack remarks scornfully that those are "kids' names," and announces that he prefers to be called by his last name, Merridew.

Jack's talent for leadership must not be overlooked. When Ralph is calling all the boys together at the first meeting,

Jack marches his choir up in a body. Since the boys were scattered all over the island when they landed, the choir must have been scattered, too, but Jack has already managed to round up the boys he is responsible for. To simply name Jack as the Evil One, or Satan, is to miss the significance of his character. At the start of the story, Jack is co-operative, if rough and positive in his behavior, and he takes a liking to Ralph. It is probably more accurate to say that Jack is a spontaneous, unthinking person, and that he represents the unconscious part of the mind, as suggested by the "madness" in his eyes, and by his bloodlust. From another point of view, a "satanic" reading of the novel, Jack can be regarded as an existential hero: he wants gratification of his desires *here* and *now*. He does not live for some vague future, like Ralph, but rather lives each day as though it were the only day. He is not an immoral character, or even an anti-moral one; he is amoral. He recognizes no morality except what can be enforced. If he is in power and can enforce his will, he has no qualms about such abstractions as "right," or "justice."

Piggy

He comes from the working class. He lived with his aunt, who kept a sweet shop, clearly, a British lower-middle-class background. His father is dead and his mother is an unknown quantity. His background contrasts with Ralph's, who comes from a "good" family. Piggy's physical appearance and his health both militate against him. He is fat and "bald-looking," with his thin hair that never seems to grow (he never becomes savage) as if he were an old man. He also has asthma, and weak eyes, both of which are common afflictions of age. These physical weaknesses and characteristics are consistent with the adult role he plays in the novel. Piggy is a clear thinker. Even Ralph has to admit that he cannot think the way Piggy can. However, Piggy cannot enforce his will as Ralph or Jack can, for he is ludicrous in appearance and the boys refuse to take him seriously. The only way Piggy is able to make himself heard at all is by explaining to Ralph what should be done and why. If Piggy can convince Ralph that a course of action is sensible, then Ralph will implement the idea. Piggy and Jack are almost diametrical opposites. Jack takes an instant dislike to Piggy, calling him "Fatty," and telling him to shut up. Jack does not want to hcar Piggy talk because Piggy always makes sense and Jack much prefers to act upon impulse. Unlike Jack, Piggy is never impulsive. He does have animal appetites, however, as indicated by his excessive fatness, a sign that he likes to eat. It is Piggy who suggests to Ralph in Chapter 9 that they go to the feast Jack is preparing, ostensibly "to make sure nothing happens," as he explains it, but actually to get a piece of the roast meat. Piggy's role in the novel is heavily symbolic. He represents the force of reason among the boys, and his gradual loss of sight and, finally, his loss of life itself, are used as a yardstick to measure the progressive degeneration of the boys.

Simon

He is an intended Christ figure in the novel. Even his physical appearance seems to echo descriptions and paintings of Jesus. He is a small, thin boy with a pointed chin and very bright eyes. He has long, coarse black hair over a low, broad forehead. He goes barefoot, as Jesus is supposed to have. Simon is very co-operative. He is the only boy who helps Ralph build the shelters. Even the sensible Piggy, who probably had good suggestions to make concerning the building, does not help with the actual work. He is seen stretched out on the beach while Ralph and Simon sweat over the huts. It might be worth mentioning that Jesus was a carpenter, a builder, that is, suggesting a further parallel. But Simon seems to prefer the natural house over the man-made one. He likes to slip out at night, when the others are sleeping in the shelters, to a vine- and creeper-covered place in the jungle, where he perhaps meditates. Simon, unlike Piggy, has intuitive wisdom. The other boys think he is "cracked" because they cannot understand him. His intelligence, like Jesus', goes beyond the immediately visible. He is able to foretell Ralph's eventual rescue, and so provide Ralph with some needed assurance. This reassurance stays with Ralph even during the final harrowing hunt, when he is enclosed by the savage boys, in Chapter 12. When a savage is trying to see Ralph in his hiding place, Ralph tells himself not to scream and that he will be rescued, remembering a phrase of comfort from the dead Simon, so his words are shown to be still living and serving their purpose. Simon's high level of intuitive intelligence is best seen in the interview with the Lord of the Flies, where Simon comes to see that the beast is in all the boys. Simon is fearfully shy and fearfully brave. He cannot speak at all in front of a group of boys. His words of wisdom are not heard, thus suggesting that the mystic, the prophet, will always be treated as an eccentric, and will be ignored. Simon's bravery is evidenced by his going to his private hiding place in the jungle at night, a time when the other boys are afraid to go out, but above all, by his dramatic confrontation with the "beast." Simon forces his feet to walk him right up to the dead airman, even though he does not know that he will survive the experience. Simon represents that part of man which is sensitive to beauty and truth.

Roger

He is a mystery. Very little information is given about him. Nothing of his background is mentioned, and his thought processes are barely touched upon twice. All we can say about him must be judged by inference. He is a "slight, furtive" boy with black hair and a low forehead, much given to secrecy. He mutters his name when asked, almost as though he does not care to give out even that little information about himself. He is a fitting lieutenant for Jack, for he is as mindless of consequences as Jack. This absence of logic can be seen in Chapter 4, when a number of coconuts fall in a circle around Roger. He might have been seriously injured, or even killed by a direct blow from one of the nuts, but he does not think of that. Instead, he connects the falling of the nuts around him with the application he sees in it and starts to throw stones so as to just miss hitting Henry.

Roger, whose name means "famous with the spear," lives up to his name in the sordid sow-killing when he performs the unnecessarily cruel part of driving his spear into the dying creature's rear-end. Roger's interest in inflicting pain marks him as sadistic. He appears to derive a measure of sexual gratification from his cruelty. By the end of the novel, Roger has become a murderer. He tips the rock over on Piggy with a sense of "delirious abandonment." As a torturer, Roger's influence becomes so ominous that he seems to even surpass Jack, as bad as he is. It is Roger who "sharpened a stick at both ends" for the execution of Ralph. Roger is the logical extension of Jack — he points the way to man's final inhumanity to man. From Golding's point of view, Roger probably constitutes a warning that if man fails to shape a peaceful society strong enough to withstand the threat of wars and dictators, he will ultimately be at the mercy of those who show no mercy.

Samneric

They are a pair of light blond, identical twins. They are without identity as separate individuals. They do everything together, and they even seem to share the same thoughts. When they talk, they split up their conversation, finishing each other's sentences and phrases. Samneric are so much alike that they look blurred, as though it is hard to tell where one boy leaves off and the other begins. Their rule is to serve whomever is the leader. They work cheerfully for Ralph in Chapter 2, helping gather wood for a fire, but when Jack paints his face and orders the twins to hunt with him, in Chapter 4, they hunt even though they are supposed to be tending the signal fire. When Jack kills his first pig at the expense of keeping the fire going, the twins are harnessed to lugging back the carcass on a pole. Chastened by Ralph, they resume their duty as fire tenders, until they mistake the airman for the "beast." Since the twins serve as muscle, as strength to be harnessed, they can be taken to represent the unthinking masses of society. These masses are peaceable, likeable and good-natured. They elect leaders like Ralph, but they lack moral conviction and they are obtuse; they lack understanding of the meaning of events. Thus, the masses of Germany allowed themselves to be coerced into supporting a dictator in the 1930's, and even became enthusiastic toward him for a time. Samneric seem to be loyal to Ralph, and show no inclination to abandon him, even after all the rest of the older boys have. But when they are captured by Jack and forced to join his band, they serve him just as faithfully. They order Ralph to leave, because they are faithfully following Jack's orders and haven't the moral courage to slip away with Ralph and make a stand at forming an outlaw band. Tortured, they reveal the very hiding place Ralph had told them about, never imagining that they would give him away. During the hunting of Ralph, he can expect no mercy from them for they are now loyal to the new chief. If the chief tells them to throw their spears at Ralph as if he were a pig, they will do it. They may stumblingly blurt out something to the effect that they don't like having to do it, but they haven't the stamina between them to revolt. The twins are the crowd, or the mass, in society. They are likeable, irresponsible, fickle.

Questions and Answers on Characters

Question 5.
Discuss the development of Ralph as the protagonist.

Answer
Ralph develops as a human being. He arrives on the island as a rather typical "boy's boy." That is, he is a good-looking, average sort of person who fits into his age group without a ripple of discord. He's fairly quiet, not especially thoughtful, and selfish without meaning to be. He just has never had to think about very serious issues, so he thinks about what is important to him. He is enthusiastic and fun loving; he stands on his head for joy at times. But when Ralph is elected chief, he is suddenly put into a position of responsibility for others. He has never had such cares before and he begins to make mistakes. He feels vaguely responsible for the disappearance of the mulberry-birthmarked boy. Then, after a while, the subject becomes forbidden, as he comes to a fuller realization of his guilt. Ralph learns from being chief that making the right decisions is extremely important, and just about impossible to do. His mistakes argue that he is not a very good leader, and Golding himself tells us that Ralph lacks Piggy's ability to think clearly and logically. Ralph's thinking does not improve. As the story progresses, he becomes increasingly forgetful. He regresses into such earlier forms of behavior as biting his fingernails and retreating from reality into a fantasy world. Does this mean that Ralph is a degenerating character rather than a developing one? No, it means that he is both at the same time. He is a degenerating character who, by the end of the novel, comes snarling out of the bushes like a wild animal, but this is a role forced upon him by others. He is degenerating because man is a degenerate animal, and Ralph is growing into manhood. Nevertheless, Ralph is a developing

character, because he can understand at the end of the story what his adventures have meant. He weeps because innocence is at an end and for the loss of his wise friend, Piggy.

Ralph has developed as a human being. The boy who stands weeping at the end of the novel will never again be the carefree person he was at the beginning. He knows too much to be free, he has seen too much to be selfish, and he has experienced too much to be trusting. He has lost his ability to believe the child's view of the world as a garden with quaintly wild fringes (the walled garden visited by wild ponies); he sees the world through adult eyes. All along, he thought his island adventure was a game. But Ralph came to see that life is for real, and its conclusion, death, is final and irrevocable.

Question 6.

Is Jack a developing character or is he static — a revealed character?

Answer

Jack's development is negative. As he moves through the novel, he becomes less and less admirable, less and less human. He learns many things, it is true, but invariably applies his knowledge in the service of his own ego. Jack is a degenerating character but, unlike Ralph, who also degenerates, he is not shown as having the redeeming quality of becoming more of a human being. One can only think that Jack is disappointed when he bursts upon the beach and sees the officer there, for now he will not get to kill Ralph.

Yet, at the opening of the novel, Jack is the one character who is shown to have a fully developed personality. This is indicated by the fact that only he of all the boys is given both a first and last name. He is firm in dealing with his choir, and businesslike in dealing with Ralph. He knows his own mind and, with his considerable experience, is sure of himself. In Chapter 2, Jack tries to allay the littl'uns' fears of a "beastie" by telling them that they are not savages and that they're Englishmen, so they must do what is right.

This indicates that Jack consciously rejects savagery in favor of civilized behavior. Jack starts as a full character, with a well-developed personality, a boy who is fussy about having his last name used, as it is more "grownup." But he ends by becoming nameless and is finally known only as "the Chief."

He has degenerated all the way to primitive, highly emotional behavior. He is ridden by superstition; he no longer gives any thought to doing the "right things" but uses force, torture, threats and punishment to whip all of the boys into obedience to his rule. He is like a dictator who sets out to conquer the world and swallow it whole. Jack's love of hunting is connected with his compulsion to kill, a tendency that Golding believes all men share. It is this bloodlust, once awakened, which starts man on the road to degeneracy.

Question 7.

Contrast Piggy and Simon.

Answer

Both Piggy and Simon are static — that is, revealed — characters who are not shown as changed by their experience. Piggy is still indefatigably Piggy up until the moment of his death. He is still using logic and reason; he is still talking. Simon cannot be said to change either. He is more fully revealed to us in Chapter 8, when he talks with the Lord of the Flies, but his understanding has been very advanced all along. As early as Chapter 5, Simon has grasped the problem of fear, and recognized that the boys are afraid of themselves. Piggy and Simon are not subject to development because they are primarily symbolic figures. Piggy represents reason and Simon represents intuitive wisdom. These two characters serve as extensions of thought and feeling in the other characters, rather than individuals in their own right. And they are removed from the story by death when it is time to show that what they represent no longer exists on the island.

Both reason and intuition are qualities highly prized by the author. He shows that few people either have or can recognize in others such attributes. The level-headed Ralph is well enough equipped mentally to be able to see that Piggy has brains, so he listens to Piggy's ideas. But no one else does (except at the beginning, when Piggy harangues the boys for nearly setting the island on fire). And no one listens to Simon at all. Symbolically speaking, this inability to understand Simon is what brings ruin to the island community. Golding is very pessimistic here, for he is saying that mankind is deaf to the voices of its prophets (probably its poets and philosophers) and this is why man is forever making the same costly mistakes, over and over again. Even Ralph regards Simon as "cracked."

Since reason is primarily associated by Golding with man's attempt to form a rational society, Piggy is shown as a social being. He fears being alone, enjoys being surrounded by people. He loves to talk and, of course, there must be other people in order for there to be conversation. Piggy dislikes manual labor, a characteristic that connects with his view that life is "scientific," for science seeks to ease man's work.

Since Simon's symbolic role is to suggest the qualities of intuitive wisdom, he is presented as uneasy in social situations. He is almost unable to speak from shyness when he is in a meeting. Since he derives his wisdom from looking within himself, rather than from the external world, he is shown as being a retiring sort of person who seems to actually prefer being alone to being with others. This does not mean that he is socially irresponsible, for he is not. On the contrary, he is the only boy who faithfully helps Ralph with the work of building the shelters. But while he recognizes and performs his duty to society, he goes off by himself when his work is done, and he even prefers sleeping alone in the forest to sleeping in the more secure shelters. Piggy is physically a coward, but mentally brave. Simon is brave in both ways.

Question 8.
What is the advantage of using boys as characters?

Answer
The boys, with their outward innocence and inner corruption, represent, quite readily, the theme of the existence of evil in man. Much of the irony in the novel derives from the discrepancy between pleasant appearances and horrible realities. Even the relatively civilized boys, Piggy and Ralph, join in the slaughter of their friend, Simon.

Question 9.
What is the meaning of Simon's encounter with the Lord of the Flies?

Answer
Simon, who represents the highest aspirations of the human spirit towards beauty and holiness, participates in a

symbolic dialogue with the Lord of the Flies, who represents the lowest part of man, the source of violence, hatred, fear, murder. The meeting represents the recognition of these forces in all men, even the saintly. The episode refutes benevolent and optimistic theories of man and the universe.

Meaning

There are as many meanings to a work of art as there are ways of looking at it. When we paraphrase a story without retelling the action we are talking about meaning. Any given meaning is an abstraction based upon the tendencies shown by specific events. But it should be kept in mind that these tendencies must be seen in terms of the total action. To abstract a meaning from a minor detail can be fatally erroneous. Thus, if we were to abstract from the first chapter of *Lord of the Flies*, the "meaning" we would get would be absurdly contradictory to the total meaning of the novel. We would be saying that *Lord of the Flies* is a story about a group of boys who had a lot of fun on a deserted island; that they elect a chief and are happy having adventures together. Thus, while it is possible to break down structure and character into chapters, discussing meaning in this fashion can be very misleading. It is necessary always to keep the total drift of the story in mind in order to make valid statements about meaning. A fundamental lesson in how to understand a novel is also contained here. Just as the meaning relates to the overall tendencies of the story, so it should be apparent that it is not possible to make any statements regarding meaning until the entire novel has been read and digested, right to the last word of the last page. The novelist is manipulating characters, plot and situation all along, and he can cause his story to work out any way he wants it to. The reader should suspend his judgment altogether as he reads through the first time. He should notice as many details, plot devices and character traits as possible along the way, but he should never begin forming conclusions concerning what these tendencies add up to until all the facts are in. As can be seen, the best way to read any novel is to read through with a completely open mind, draw whatever conclusions seem to be warranted by the story, and then *read it again*.

1. Explaining the Themes

It is helpful to bear in mind that novels are complex pieces of writing which have more than one meaning. Any pattern of consistent tendencies found in a novel constitutes a theme. There are many themes in *Lord of the Flies*. To isolate and discuss any of these is to talk about one aspect of the meaning

68

of the book. Much of the action in *Lord of the Flies* can be examined in terms of the theme of fear: how it operates and what it does to people. Other themes of the novel have to do with war and peace, the nature of society, civilization, human hope, the fall of man, primitivism, leadership and so on. Any one of these themes can be isolated for examination. Theoretically, the meaning of a novel should be the summation of the meanings of its themes, but since it is impossible ever to encompass all of the threads of meaning in a good novel, it is also difficult ever to be in a position to state dogmatically, "*This* is *the* meaning of the novel."

2. Methods of Analysis

Professional literary critics employ a wide range of approaches to their craft, to the business, that is, of getting at meaning. Some of these methods seem to be more fruitful in dealing with certain novels, while different methods seem to work better with others. A number of approaches have been used in the commentary section, as a means of indicating the wide range of different meanings suggested by the author. Some critics believe that "pure" criticism is arrived at by using only one method of analysis and sticking strictly to that. Others believe that the best method is to use as many critical approaches as seem appropriate.

3. Biographical Criticism

This is used to explain a story in terms of its relation to the life of the author. Some novels can only be understood in this fashion, but it is not much help with *Lord of the Flies*. The only connections we can observe are rather sketchy, and do not explain much. Golding was a naval officer during World War II, a fact which may or may not connect with the boys' rescue by a naval officer. Golding was a grammar school teacher who was in daily contact with small boys. This experience certainly has a direct bearing upon the novel inasmuch as the author knows little boys well enough to write well about them. But there is no plot parallel here.

4. Historical Criticism

This is employed when the analysis places the events of the novel in their historical setting. Helpful in many cases, this method is again of little service with *Lord of the Flies*, as the action takes place in the future. Thus, we have no basis for comparing it with actual history. About all we can do here is compare the wartime background of the novel with World War II.

5. Comparative Criticism

This is used when the novel in question is examined in terms of its possible relationship with other novels or stories on the same theme, or dealing with the same events, or by the same author. A great deal can be done with this approach, and Golding himself mentions the titles of other stories to which his might be compared. The deliberate contrast set up with *The Coral Island* has been mentioned in the Introduction. But *Treasure Island* and *Swallows and Amazons* are also mentioned. There is even mention that the beast may swing through the trees like "what's its name," a shadowy reference to *Tarzan of the Apes*. This comparative approach to meaning can yield interesting results.

6. Psychological Criticism

As its name suggests, this is concerned with explaining why things happen. This method leans heavily upon character analysis and motivation. Much of the commentary in this study is psychological in approach. Applied to the overall conclusion which *Lord of the Flies* seems to urge, psychological criticism yields statements about man as an unthinking, unfeeling and bloodthirsty "beast."

7. Social or Cultural Criticism

This method seeks to relate a novel to the culture from which it springs. This method is especially useful where the novel seems to be making a number of comments upon how people live and behave. Satirists like William Golding can be shown to be really talking about their own world, and criticizing it, when they cause their fictional characters to act out their make-believe lives. The naval officer who looks with satisfaction at his "trim cruiser" is far removed from the ragged little boys who made such a mess of the island. He is neat and orderly, dignified and civilized. But he is in the business of killing, just like Jack and Roger. So the naval officer becomes a representative of modern man in the world, and a social comment is made which insists that in the real world, not just in the world of the novel, men delude themselves with outward shows of manner and custom into thinking they are a great deal more sensible and humane than they really are.

Questions and Answers on Meaning

Question 10.
What is the primary meaning of *Lord of the Flies*?

Answer
The meaning of *Lord of the Flies* is its description of the nature of man. About this Golding, himself, has written:

> The theme is an attempt to trace the defects of society back to the defects of human nature. The moral is that the shape of a society must depend on the ethical nature of the individual and not on any political system however apparently logical or respectable. The whole book is symbolic in nature except the rescue in the end where adult life appears, dignified and capable, but in reality enmeshed in the same evil as the symbolic life of the children on the island. The officer, having interrupted a manhunt, prepares to take the children off the island in a cruiser which will presently be hunting its enemy in the same implacable way. And who will rescue the adult and his cruiser?

The novel runs directly contrary to the belief that naturally good man is the innocent and helpless victim of social forces over which he has no control. The world is the way it is because the people in it are the way they are, says Golding, rather than the converse. Golding is in the minority, it must be noted, for the large majority of modern writers and thinkers, clinging to Rousseau's ideal of the noble savage — natural man as good by instinct — are committed to the position that man is victimized from birth by society, which is the real culprit.

Golding's position is a very old one. It goes back at least as far as the Old Testament. In the first book, the Book of

Genesis, Adam and Eve are presented as having brought their own downfall upon themselves through disobedience (they were not to seek knowledge of good and evil). This disobedience has been called Original Sin. And theologians have long taught that all of mankind is sinful and wicked because Adam and Eve were. From this point of view, man is born into the world in a state of original sin, a fault directly traceable to his own human nature, and not to society. It is clear from the novel, as well as from what Golding has indicated, concerning his intentions in the book, that he shares a common conviction with those who believe in the fall of man. This does not mean that Golding shares the religious point of view that Christianity builds upon that initial thesis, for he does not. Golding is often erroneously herded into various camps of religious orthodoxy to which he does not belong. There is a coincidence of meaning here, rather than a borrowing, or any dependency upon a supernatural frame of reference. For, Golding specifically indicates all through his novel that no actual magic is to be imagined as existing. A reading of *The Inheritors* erases any confusion on this point. *The Inheritors* follows directly after publication of *Lord of the Flies*, and again attacks the problem of understanding the primitive mind. The Neanderthal man is Golding's answer to the myth of the Garden of Eden. Golding presents his primitive apelike man as a much nicer person than modern man. He is not fallen, he is not wicked; he would never organize a warlike society as Jack did. And that is why he no longer exists. He was too gentle, too nice to survive, Golding indicates. For, survival in the world as we know it is defined as having struggled and overcome. Thus, the qualities of survivors will be toughness, rather than gentleness. Out of this surviving humanity comes the individual who is hard enough to exist in the world, and who ruthlessly takes for himself what he wants, even at the expense of the well-being of others. There can be no happy solution to the problems of man's society because "the defects of human nature" shape society after their own imperfections.

Question 11.

Discuss the theme of fear in connection with the overall meaning of the novel.

Answer

Golding manages to achieve a great unity of purpose through his uses of fear in *Lord of the Flies*. Fear is perhaps the most convincing single emotion he could have chosen, for everyone has fears and every adult can remember certain childhood fears. The universality of this emotion provides its prime power. Golding's master stroke is to present fear as the motive power behind the actions of the boys, for the validity of the emotion gives validity to the motivation. Ralph foolishly climbs the mountain at night in search of the beast. Why he does this is the patent absurdity that he fears being accused of cowardice! As the boys degenerate, their fears become increasingly powerful and increasingly irrational. They are becoming afraid of things they would not have thought of a few months earlier. A number of taboos arise. The mulberry-birthmarked boy is never mentioned. Snakes are not mentioned. Later on, Jack's name becomes a taboo word and is used no more. After the "beast" is seen, it too becomes taboo. The fear demonstrated by these taboos is quite irrational. It amounts to a superstition that the thing named is the thing itself. The primitive mind is full of such beliefs. And, of course, as the boys lose their hold on their former civilized ways, they tend to fall more and more into this fallacy.

The major meaning of Golding's novel is contained in this progression of fear, from the fear of the imagined beast to the fear of nothing at all — taboos, mere words — superstition as the governing force over human behavior. For these fears shape the individual. What does one do when his fears become absurd? According to William Golding, such fears turn man against man, for he cannot trust anyone when he does not know what or who he is afraid of. This is signalled by the mounting distrust between Jack and Ralph, a distrust that always flares up on the question of bravery, or perhaps more accurately, fear of cowardice. Fear is so predominant that neither boy can bear to be thought of as a coward. The ultimate manifestation of the mutual distrust of man against man is violence. And this is the ugly conclusion the novel moves towards. The problem of the writer is to establish the nature of man as being naturally fearful, then put him in a situation that feeds his fears, then show fearful man as distrusting his fellows, then dividing for security (Jack doesn't think Ralph is a good leader) and, finally, trying to get rid of the fear by destroying everyone or everything that one is afraid of. This last method can never work, because what one is really afraid of is not other people — they merely objectify the fear — it is oneself. The reason Golding has to take a pessimistic view of man in this novel is that man is primitive. He does, to this day, set out to kill other men. Until he can control his fears and recognize that killing people is not the same as killing fear, there can be no peace.

Question 12.

How do innocence and experience connect thematically with meaning, in *Lord of the Flies*?

Answer

Golding's South Sea Island permits him to make a running parallel with the proverbial Garden of Eden, the place of innocence. From this garden, Adam and Eve were expelled when they lost their innocence. As mentioned in the Introduction, Golding's island is not really a paradise, since it is visited by storms, the fruit causes diarrhea, the fallen tree trunks are rotten, the coconuts look like skulls. What Golding has done is more realistic in detail than the Old Testament story, which describes a place of perfection. The couple in Eden were innocent one day and experienced the next. This, too, is unrealistic. Golding's boys, on the other hand, lose whatever innocence they had at the beginning gradually, rather than all at once. Ralph weeps "for the end of innocence," but not because he has just that minute realized this loss. He has been realizing it all along, but he has not been able to allow himself the luxury of tears. As early as Chapter 5 he told the boys that "Things are breaking up," so he has known for months that his dream of an island paradise is not coming true.

But Ralph's understanding, his experience, is not complete until the death of Piggy, a deliberate act of murder, and his own flight from the little savages. Until Piggy's death, Ralph had been able to convince himself that the boys were just playing. This attitude reflects his relative innocence. Even Jack had said he didn't want to "play" anymore, so Jack's leaving Ralph seemed to be play also, even if Jack decided to play by his own rules. But the line between make-believe and reality began to dissolve. For Jack, it dissolved when he became the chief. Then the game suddenly became real. Drunk with power, he allowed himself to succumb to all his appetites and, the farther he went, the more he entered upon a kind of terrible reality. Ralph, who was more of a dreamer all along, was able to retain a measure of balance that served to make the savagery seem unreal, and so blinded him to the fact that Jack had ceased to play savage and had in fact become one.

The climactic action of the novel, which replaces innocence with experience, is the sow-killing. This action is caused to take place directly after Jack has split the island community by leaving Ralph and, naming himself chief, taking the hunters with him. Evidently, Golding shows these two events together in the same chapter because he wants to indicate that Jack's rebellion is like Adam's disobedience: both lead to experience. In the Old Testament, the experience seems to be sexual, for the expulsion from Eden is followed directly in the next verse by the words "And Adam knew Eve, his wife; and she conceived Cain. . . ." The loss of innocence is likened to the loss of a child's world of play and make-believe and sheltered gardens. In *Lord of the Flies*, Jack leaves Ralph and immediately goes hunting. Then follows the killing of the sow, which, as mentioned in the above, is described in sexual imagery. Of the meaning of this experience Claire Rosenfield writes:

> In this new society [the taboo] replaces the authority
> of the parents, whom the children symbolically kill
> when they slay the nursing sow. Now every kill
> becomes a sexual act, is a metaphor for childhood
> sexuality, an assertion of freedom from mores they
> had been taught to revere.

To E.L. Epstein, another critic, the sow-killing is symbolic of the legend of Oedipus, the legendary Greek ruler who unwittingly killed his father and married his mother:

> The entire incident [of the sow-killing] is a horrid
> parody of an Oedipal wedding night and these

emotions, the sensations aroused by murder and death, and the overpowering and unaccustomed emotions of sexual love experienced by the half-grown boys, release the forces of death and the devil on the island.

William R. Mueller, another critic, takes the view that the sow becomes a figure for Beelzebub. He regards the successive hunts which the boys make as trips into the nature of man. Each hunt, he contends, carries the reader closer to "natural man." When the sow's head is left mounted on a stick, Golding calls it the Lord of the Flies. Mueller observes that the Hebrew word "Beelzebub" means "lord of insects," or, as Golding has translated it, "lord of the flies." Mueller also points out that Milton, in *Paradise Lost*, names Beelzebub as second in power only to Satan.

It should be seen, however, that the Lord of the Flies is not a supernatural figure as Golding uses him. Rather, he is the lord of rot and decay. There is no magic in him. Simon correctly identifies him as a "Pig's head on a stick." He has been on the island all along, just as he has been everywhere all along. Simon is able to recognize this degenerative principle in the world, and this is symbolized when he "talks with" the sow's head. He recognizes that this principle is present in everyone, and has been from the start.

Ralph, Piggy and Samneric are absent from this hunt (as is the watching Simon). Thus, it can be said that they retain a measure of innocence that Jack and his followers lose through their highly symbolic encounter with the sow. For, whether the sow is regarded as mother, as parents, or as the figure for death and decay as a universal principle, the experience which the boys have transforms them. They become brutal savages from that time forth. They have lost their innocence.

Question 13.

What does Golding seem to be saying about human destiny?

Answer

At first glance, the future seems gray. Society is disintegrating. Anarchy and violence thrive at the expense of reason. At the end of *Lord of the Flies*, however, there is some hope for the future in the new knowledge that Ralph has acquired. He understands the conflict of good and evil, ideal and real, that exists in man. And, unlike Simon and Piggy, he is resourceful enough to elude death and to carry this knowledge back to civilization, there to have some influence on his fellow man. He will be a wise leader when he is an adult. He will be a man of reason, but also a man aware of the darkness lurking in the most innocent person. And he will have some positive effect on civilization.

Style

Style is a subject of infinite dimension. It is the HOW of writing, concerned less with what the writer has to say than with his methods of communicating. Every skilful writer has a style of his own, one which is different from every other style. In some cases, these differences are so great as to be instantly recognizable. In other cases, they are quite subtle. The style of Ernest Hemingway does not resemble that of William Faulkner. Even a glance at the two styles reveals the short, simple sentence structure Hemingway prefers, as contrasted to the very long, convoluted sentences of Faulkner. The two do not even look the same on the page. Style has to do with the way a writer puts words and sentences together. His word choice lies at the heart of his style, and whole books have been written analyzing and explaining why a writer chose this word rather than that one.

Since style is concerned with how writing is written, rather than with what is said (although the two are to some extent inseparable), style can be analyzed by asking questions and answering them about the actual sentence structure and word choice. Why did the author say it this way? Why did he use this particular word instead of some other? What is the purpose of this image, or that comparison? Does the author often use the same device? the same image? Answers to these questions are comments on the style of the author.

1. Imagery

Behind most styles is the image. Every writer seeks to create word pictures which will communicate some idea or attitude. Words which make a direct appeal to any of the five senses are images. Most images are visual, since it is easier to describe a thing in its appearance than in its smell, taste, touch or sound. We can visualize "dog" pretty easily, or "collie," or we can describe the animal "dog" in greater detail, giving its size, shape and color. But how can we describe the smell of a dog? This is not easy to do. About all that can be done with words is to say that the dog smells like something else the reader may be familiar with, or say that the smell is sharp, or musty, or pungent. But these words do not create a smell the way the word "collie" creates an image. This difficulty explains why the vast majority of images are visual.

As might be guessed, images are created largely by the use of common nouns, since they name concrete objects. Abstract nouns like "honor" or "courage" do not provide images. Proper nouns, like "Daria," summon forth the image of the particular person or thing named. William Golding uses many color images in his symbolism. Thus, colors like red, yellow, black, green, pearl and so on acquire meaning because of the ways they are used. The image becomes, as it so often does, a symbol.

2. Figurative Language

Every writer seeks to describe or to communicate moods by the use of language devices which compare one thing to another. The choice of comparisons is the author's, but every writer will have a tendency to select what seems appropriate to *him*. Thus, a "style" emerges simply because the author tends to see things in his own unique way. Two of the most versatile tools available to the writer are the metaphor and the simile. They are essentially alike. The only difference is that the simile is a stated comparison, while with a metaphor the comparison is only implied. Here is Golding's description of the coming storm, while Simon sleeps off his fit in the jungle:

> He lay in the mat of creepers while the evening advanced and the cannon continued to play.

The "cannon" refers to thunder, an implied comparison. If Golding had written "and the thunder boomed *like* cannon," he would have written a simile. Here is Simon walking "with glum determination *like* an old man," a stated comparison, therefore a simile.

3. Emphasis

This has to do with artistic proportion. In good literature, the artist is going to devote the greatest amount of space to the subjects he is most interested in. This proportion is not always exact. A character's relative importance cannot be determined by the mere counting of lines. Sometimes, dramatic effect is achieved by various delaying tactics which reduce the space devoted to a given character. The fact that Simon is killed three chapters before the end of the novel does not detract from his importance in the story. But it is generally true that the chief issues receive the greatest amount of attention. In *Lord of the Flies*, Ralph and Jack are the only two characters who appear in every chapter. This is proportionately consistent with the novel's emphasis upon those two characters. Simon appears in every chapter until his death, and Piggy does also, with the significant exception that he is absent from the quest for the beast. Emphasis is being handled consistently here; the lesser characters receive proportionately less attention.

4. Satire

Satire is a deliberate and systematic criticism of a subject, accomplished by poking fun at that subject. Humor is used as a device for ridiculing the particular faults and weaknesses the author wants to condemn. The satirist has a positive or constructive side to his endeavor, however, for his purpose in mocking is to expose wrongs as a means of suggesting ways of correcting them. But the positive dimension of satire is almost never explicitly stated; rather, it is implied. Upon the reader is placed the burden of deciding from the nature of the fault what the corrective should be. In most cases, the constructive suggestion is instantly obvious, and for the author to explain it would be to belabor the story and weaken its artistry.

5. Sentence Structure

The English language employs two fundamental sentence structures in three basic styles of writing. The sentences may be either loose or periodic. The styles may be formal, informal, or colloquial.

The loose sentence occurs most often in English. It is the basic structure of speech and of most writing. The loose sentence is so called because it puts the subject first, verb next, and then just adds on the modifiers afterwards. The more modifiers are added, the looser the sentence structure gets. This type of sentence goes all the way back to Anglo-Saxon, the parent tongue of modern English. The periodic sentence, on the other hand, is modelled after the structure of Latin and follows Latin rules of grammar. In this type of sentence, the meaning is suspended until the end of the sentence by withholding either the subject, the verb, or both.

This device produces a "tight" sentence structure:

> With some positive action before them, a little of the
> tension died.

In this sentence, the last two words are the subject, "tension," and verb "died." You must read all the way through the sentence to find out what is being talked about. The sentence which follows is a loose one:

> Ralph said no more, did nothing, stood looking down
> at the ashes around his feet.

The subject, "Ralph," is given at once and the three verbs, "said," "did" and "stood" are given immediately after.

Sentences may be formal, informal or colloquial. Formal sentences tend to be rather long and are often periodic in structure. The words used are chosen with great precision from the vocabulary which derives from Latin and Greek roots. Contractions like "He can't" for "he cannot" are not used, and the formal style is almost always written in the third person. It tends to be very obective. Scholarly articles in the learned journals are written in formal style. This is not a spoken language, since careful rewriting is necessary to achieve this level of language. Informal English, on the other hand, is modelled on the loose sentence and accounts for most of the writing in English. It also occurs in the speech of educated persons. Simpler language is used, and fewer polysyllabic words than in formal style. Contractions are used, and any pronoun person can be used. Colloquial style is the daily spoken language we all use. It usually occurs in writing only when there are characters who speak lines of dialogue. Colloquial style is full of clichés, common idiomatic expressions of the language, slang and incomplete or fragmented sentences. Writers like Kerouac, in *On the Road* or *The Dharma Bums*, are trying to write colloquially.

Questions and Answers on Style

Question 14.

What kinds of images are used in *Lord of the Flies*, and what are they used for?

Answer

Most of the images of *Lord of the Flies* are from nature, since the island is an uncivilized place. The dominant visual images are the mountain, the jungle, Castle Rock, the beach and the lagoon. In Chapter 7, the open sea is briefly glimpsed, blue and "clipped." These topographical images provide the setting for the various actions, and each is appropriate to the kinds of activities the boys engage in there. The mountain, with its signal fire, is at the opposite end of the island from Castle Rock, where fire is used only for cooking.

Images of heat and color also abound. The tropical island is steaming hot, and Golding seldom lets us forget this. He stresses the temperature in scenes of great emotion or drama. Thus, Simon's imaginary conversation with the Lord of the Flies occurs in heat that "threatened." He is sweating and very thirsty, a preparation for the coming on of Simon's fit. Again, when the boys make the first fire, which Golding wants to show is too large to be maintained and is dangerous, his method is through the use of heat images. The boys are exhausted by the fierce fire, as though by a fierce but short-lived passion to be rescued. And, of course, the climax of the novel is the hottest of all, for the boys have set the whole island on fire, and Ralph is running for the beach, the savages on one side of him and the raging fire on the other. The heat also causes images itself. When the boys are on the beach they are accustomed to seeing mirages. Sometimes, the lagoon seems to rise into the air. Other times, the whole island looks as if it will float away. These mirages are caused by heat waves lifting off the surrounding coral reef and the lagoon. They contrast with the cool water of the other side of the island, where there are no mirages.

Ralph, who dreams of a happy future, prefers the side where the mirages are, where the impossible can be dreamed of. Jack is familiar with the open sea side, where hope seems to be dead. This is consistent with Golding's purpose, for he presents Jack as the one who forgets about rescue first, and who prefers living each day without thought of the future.

Color images are used with careful consistency. Red and black are Jack's colors. He has red hair and never stops wearing the black cap. In fact, it is on his head when the naval officer stops the hunt. Ralph's color is yellow, the color of the sun. Simon's are pearl, opal and, after his death, silver: all rather luminous colors, suggestive of his role in the novel. The coral island itself is pink, a color that we associate with babies, or the pigs on the island. This color stands in ironic contrast to the action. It makes every atrocity stand out all the more terribly.

Question 15.
Discuss the use of metaphor and simile in *Lord of the Flies.*

Answer
Golding's metaphors and similes, unlike the rest of his imagery, are often taken from the civilized world. These figures of speech are used to relate the appearances and actions of the boys to the implied meaning of the novel, by suggesting comparisons with civilization. Thus, the island itself is "boat-shaped," a metaphor which likens the island to a man-made object. The first rock rolled at Ralph in Chapter 12 is a "red rock," but the second one is "half as big as a cottage, big as a car, a tank." It moves like a "steam-roller," a "mill-wheel." These comparisons liken the rock, a specimen of nature, to various man-made objects. The destructiveness of the boys' activities is suggested here, as it is in the first rock rolling on the island when, in Chapter 1, Ralph, Jack and Simon rolled a big one down the mountainside, just for fun. That time the rock rolled along "like an enraged monster," and one of the boys cried out excitedly, "Like a bomb!" The use of these similes and metaphors serves to remind the reader that while the action of the novel takes place on a remote South Sea Island, the modern world is not to be forgotten. The purpose of the novel is to illuminate the real world by means of the fictional island.

Probably the most outstanding metaphors of *Lord of the Flies* have to do with imagery of the beast. When Simon confronted the Lord of the Flies, the flies around the head "buzzed like a saw." Later, the head starts expanding "like a balloon." It talks to Simon "in the voice of a schoolmaster." All of these similes draw their images from the civilized world. In contrast to Simon's civilized vision of the "pig's head on a stick" as a schoolmaster, consider the beast as seen by Samneric. They see the dead airman not as a product of a man-made world, but as one of the natural world, if the natural world is defined as including uncataloged monsters. They see a preposterous beast with wings, claws, teeth, "slinking behind the trees" after them. The contrast these metaphors show reveals Golding's purpose. The twins are afraid of nature, and incorrectly; for they only fear the monsters that superstition encourages them to believe in. The real threat is carried in metaphors having to do with man and his inventions. The Lord of the Flies speaks in the voice of a schoolmaster when it says that the boys are going to "do" Simon, if he doesn't forget about the beast. And, of course, they do. Man, not monsters, is man's enemy. The last spoken words of the novel are uttered by the naval officer who rescues the boys. And, again his speech uses figurative language from the civilized world:

I know. Jolly good show. Like the Coral Island.

The officer compares the fiasco of the boys' misadventures to a 19th-century novel of adventure, in which the castaway boys made a raving success of their stay on an island, even to converting a bunch of cannibals to Christianity. This simile, "like the Coral Island," is a very sophisticated one, since it is based upon a very sophisticated man-made object, a book, and is meaningless except to people who are familiar with that particular book. Thus, the simile and metaphor have been ingeniously employed in this novel as a means for providing the perspective of comparison with civilization. And, since the metaphor and simile are used for comparison, there is a harmony in the use of these details with the total intentions of the novelist.

Question 16.
Discuss the uses of satire in *Lord of the Flies*.

Answer
Since Golding's purpose in writing his novel is to "trace the defects of society back to the defects of human nature," his aim is really to comment upon the civilized world. His boys are merely the metaphor by means of which he makes his comments upon the real world. His metaphor is itself satirical, since it makes fun of adults. Briefly put, *Lord of the Flies* says that civilized man in his civilized society is no better than a

pack of children running wild without adult supervision. The comparison seems absurd, at first, so there is humor in it. But Golding does a pretty good job of making his argument stick. That naval officer at the end of the story is too close to the reality of the warlike world we all know to be ignored. He looks and talks like a gentleman, polished and sophisticated. But, in the line of his duty, he will find the enemy and give the order to commence firing, killing indiscriminately whatever men his shells or depth charges explode upon. Thus, despite appearances to the contrary, the officer is *really* a killer. And, so, by a weird twist, Golding shows us that the hated Jack really is the chief; that he and not Ralph symbolizes the leadership of the "civilized" world. This is a satirical comparison because it mocks the adults of the world. None of them would be likely to admit that they are at all like Jack. They would certainly identify with Ralph, who is not a leader as leaders *are* in the world, but rather as we want to believe leaders *should be*. And there is a world of difference between what is (reality) and what should be (our dreams, our ideals).

A great many instances of satire occur in the novel. Some are only funny in a bitter way. They employ what has come to be known as "black humor," a kind of humor that is only funny because it reveals a terrible truth we do not like to face. Consider Roger's narrow escape in Chapter 4, as the heavy coconuts rain down all around him. Roger should be very glad he was lucky enough not to have had his head broken, but this thought never occurs to him. Instead, he sees that he might try throwing stones at Henry so as to just miss hitting him, the way the coconuts had just missed Roger. Here, the satire is obvious. Roger has had instruction offered him on the subject of change, luck and good fortune; but he misses the point completely. This incident suggests that man typically turns the potential lessons of nature into channels of destruction. Instead of learning to preserve and cherish when he sees the lightning bolt strike, man instead learns that *he* wants a lightning bolt to throw.

Satire of a more obviously humorous sort appears when Ralph and Piggy talk in Chapter 10 with Samneric about the "dance" at which Simon was killed. None of the boys admits having been there, even though they are all scarred and obviously shaken by the terrible experience:

Memory of the dance that none of them had attended shook all four boys convulsively.

This incident contains humor, for it builds upon the game of pretending, of trying to hide what is apparent. It is satirical because the author makes us see how obvious their lies are. He is making fun of his characters as a means of suggesting the remedy: that it would be far better for the boys to undertake an honest facing of the facts, and shouldering of their own responsibility and guilt for Simon's death. That way, they might hope to forestall future calamities.

For the most part, the satire in *Lord of the Flies* is aimed at very large targets. Golding is not so much interested in the smaller human traits, such as those illustrated. Rather, he aims for the social animal, mass man, as his chief target. By showing the boys as essentially mindless "followers" of whomever is leading them, the author satirizes the civilized voters of democracies and the citizens of voteless dictatorships as being followers too, who, sheeplike, accept whatever they are told. They have no more conviction than Samneric, who take the easiest way out of each situation. Here, the corrective of the fault is clearly implied. The masses should not be masses. Everyone should do his own thinking. Good leaders should be given active and thoughtful help with their programs. Bad leaders should be instantly stripped of power. Above all, every man should refuse to do anything which he knows to be wrong merely because he has been ordered to do it.

Question 17.
Comment on the sentence structure of *Lord of the Flies*.

Answer
Two entirely distinct styles are employed in the sentences of this novel, informal, and colloquial. The novel consists of narrative portions alternating with dialogue, the speech of the boys themselves.

The narrative parts of the novel, those which tell the story, are written in informal English. The story is told by a narrator, presumably Golding himself. This narrator uses short sentences written in a simple, clear style. He does not try to write "elegantly," nor does he try to sound "literary." The sentences are not so short as those of Hemingway, but nearly so. Golding's informal sentences are characterized by the use of a simple vocabulary and careful selection of words. He uses understatement when he wishes to heighten the impact of his meaning. Thus, when Piggy falls to his death, the enormity of the crime is emphasized by the objective, unemotional description: "stuff came out and turned red" is a pretty mild understatement of what someone looks like when his brains have been dashed out. But this same understatement is extremely effective, for it puts greater demands upon the reader than a highly emotional style would. When a melodramatic style is used, the author is going through the emotional feeling instead of the reader. But when the style is flat, the reader is left with a feeling of inadequacy, as though not enough has been said about this terrible event. The reader is likely to react to the flat "stuff came out" by wanting to shout: "What! The poor kid has been hounded all the time he was on the island, laughed at and kidded, and then blinded by those imbeciles! Now they murder him in cold blood and all you have to say is that 'stuff came out and turned red.' That 'stuff' is blood! That poor kid never had a chance; he was treated just like some animal!" This sort of reaction is what Golding is hoping to pull forth from the reader by not putting the emotions into words himself.

The speech of the boys is colloquial. The oldest boy is only twelve, and the others are still younger. It would not make sense to have them talk like college men, or even high-school graduates. To be believable, their speech must resemble the language that such boys could be expected to use at their ages. They should make grammatical mistakes, they should use the kinds of expressions and slang English schoolboys use. They should talk in incomplete sentences and sentence fragments, as these are common to colloquial speech. Slang is used throughout the conversations. Jack, at one point, says, "He's buzzed off." This is not American slang, but it is common in England. Informally written, Jack would have to say "He's gone away." But Jack would not be a believable character if he spoke the informal style. Even Piggy, the nearest thing on the island to an intellectual, speaks colloquially. In fact, his speech is pointed out as being inferior to Ralph's and most of the other boys'. He has what they consider an accent, and he manages to get his grammar tangled around his feet when he speaks:

> Then when you get here you build a fire that isn't no
> use. Now you been and set the whole island on fire.

Piggy manages to get off a double negative in the first sentence, a common grammatical fault, but his next sentence has some variations on the language that are entirely his own. What is the English translation of "Now you been and set?" Again, the speech is realistic, and the speech of Piggy is characteristic of him. He can be depended upon to have the clearest ideas and the worst grammar spoken on the island.

*Golding's Technique

"I have made up my mind that it's capital, — first rate, — the best thing that ever happened to us, and the most splendid prospect that ever lay before three jolly young tars. We've got an island all to ourselves."

Peterkin Gay speaks these spirited words in the third chapter of *The Coral Island.* Later he says, referring again to the island on which he and his companions are wrecked, ' "My dear boys, we're set up for life; it must be the ancient Paradise — hurrah!" ' And indeed Ballantyne's three castaways live together on their island in a prelapsarian state of 'uninterrupted harmony and happiness'.

William Golding in *Lord of the Flies* (Faber and Faber, 1954) treats the same theme as Ballantyne. His chief characters are, like Ballantyne's, called Ralph and Jack; wrecked in the Pacific, they survive until they are rescued; the naval officer who saves them remarks " 'Jolly good show. Like the Coral Island.' " But *The Coral Island* is a romance, and in *Lord of the Flies* Mr. Golding reconceives Ballantyne's story in remorselessly unromantic terms.

His castaways are a party of English schoolboys whose plane has been shot down in flames. Left to govern themselves, for all the adults have been killed, they at first delight in their freedom and in the pleasures of the island. (One of them observes that it is like the Coral Island itself.) They elect as their leader a boy called Ralph, and under his guidance they agree to keep a fire burning as a signal, to summon assemblies by blowing a conch, and to allow a hearing to any boy holding the conch. Ralph and Piggy, a fat intelligent boy with asthma, arrange to build shelters, leaving foraging to a slightly older boy, Jack Merridew. As the leader of a group of choirboys who were among the castaways, he was envious of Ralph's election; to pacify him Ralph suggested that the choir, led by Jack, should undertake to hunt the wild pigs living in the forests. Jack welcomes this and says that they will also watch the fire and keep a lookout.

However, the tedious duties of providing shelter and

---

*Editor's title. From "Second Reading," by Philip Drew, *The Cambridge Review* (Oct. 27, 1956).

tending the fire soon pall, and it becomes clear that hunting is the real attraction. A ship passes, but the fire is out because the choirboys have gone hunting. Although Ralph and Piggy call frequent assemblies in which they try to rally the boys, the nerve of the party is broken by superstitious terror. When, at the last full assembly, Ralph unwisely disparages Jack's hunters, Jack goes off by himself. The rest of the novel tells how one by one the boys desert Ralph and Piggy, or are captured by the hunters and forced to join their 'tribe'. The tribe paint their faces, live under strict, almost military, discipline in a natural fortress at one end of the island, hunt the pigs by day, and leave the heads of their kill as a propitiatory gift for 'the beast'. Driven by fear, superstition and an obsession with hunting, Jack becomes increasingly tyrannical. Simon, an eccentric visionary choirboy, is done to death by the tribe in a ritual hunting dance, as he tries to tell them that they need have no fear of the beast on the mountain. Piggy is murdered by Jack's sadistic lieutenant Roger while he holds the conch, and Ralph is left alone. Goaded by Jack and Roger, all the other boys hunt him over the island, intending to sacrifice him when they catch him. They set the forest on fire, and just as Ralph must be killed either by the flames or by the spears of the hunters a cruiser sights the smoke and lands a rescue party.

Thus baldly summarised the plot sounds crude and sensational, but such is Mr. Golding's skill and discretion in its deployment that the progressive disintegration of the group and degeneration of the individual are conveyed with subtlety and fidelity. Simply as narrative *Lord of the Flies* is exceptionally exciting and moving. But a deeper significance is implicit in the undertaking, and it is this which gives the novel its singular quality. By differing so sharply from Ballantyne's account of what happens when boys are left to their own devices Mr. Golding implies a radically less sanguine view of human nature and civilization. More explicitly he uses his Pacific island to symbolize the condition of humanity. Having clinically insulated life on the island from the world and thus contrived a microcosm, he magnifies and inspects it. By this method, which is common ground to the great allegorists and satirists, he examines the problem of how to maintain moderate liberal values and to pursue distant ends against pressure from extremists and against the lower instincts.

Like the method the problem has exercised many writers of allegory and satire. In theme and treatment *Lord of the Flies* seems at first glance to resemble *1984*: in fact the books differ fundamentally. In *1984* Orwell is writing as a satirist. He is not concerned to symbolize man's condition or even the plight of modern man. His object is simply to record as forcefully as possible dangerous symptoms which he had already observed developing in Russia, America, and above all in Britain. To do this he exaggerated and extrapolated them, foreshortening the whole to bring his picture within the probable lifetime of most of his readers. *1984* is not about eternal values nor about the future of the world: it is about the sort of life we are living now. It has no allegorical or symbolic significance. To believe that it has is to weaken Orwell's satiric insistence that all the horrors of which he writes are not abstractions or imaginings but are *already* in the world. *Lord of the Flies* offers no such specific portrait of our own time. It is thus formally closer to *Animal Farm*, Orwell's timeless allegory of government, than to *1984*. It is not however the sort of allegory which depends on the establishment of neat one-for-one relationships between things inside and things outside the story.

Certain correspondences are nevertheless at once evident. For example, the conch which regulates the assemblies is a figure for the right of free speech in a free society. The fire which must be kept burning has a less rigid parallel — in the novel it represents a duty which must be done not for any immediate end but because it offers some hope of ultimate salvation. As Ralph says,

> ' "The fire is the most important thing on the island. How can we ever be rescued except by luck, if we don't keep a fire going? Is a fire too much for us to make?"
>
> 'He flung out an arm.
>
> ' "Look at us! How many are we? And yet we can't keep a fire going to make smoke. Don't you understand? Can't you see we ought to — ought to die before we let the fire out?" '   (Chapter 5)

At first the sole hope of rescue, keeping the fire alight

gradually becomes, even to Ralph himself, a symbolic duty. 'Ralph tried indignantly to remember. There was something good about a fire. Something overwhelmingly good.' (Chapter 10) In the novel attention to the onerous business of building and looking after the fire is the mark of the more mature characters. While the task of maintaining the fire is the most obvious touchstone of the boys' quality, the entire situation which Mr. Golding has devised is a test of their ability to survive by any but the most barbaric standards, and hence of the reality of civilization, and of Man's claim to be an adult creature.

Similarly the individual characters, although they are fully realised within the limits of their age, have symbolic value. Ralph and Jack are, of course, the poles of the novel. Ralph is decent, though not very intelligent, and has qualities of leadership, but it is Jack who finally dominates the other boys. He is arrogant, brave, boastful, unscrupulous and finally murderous. He and Ralph feel a continual attraction and antipathy: in the last chapter Ralph realizes this fatal truth — 'Then there was that indefinable connection between himself and Jack; who therefore would never let him alone; never.' On Ralph's side Piggy typifies thoughtfulness and intelligence, the advanced side of man's mind which has made for human survival and material development. His weakness is that he cannot convince others or convey his ideas to a general audience. When Jack steals his spectacles he at last finds words which strike home.

> 'The shape of the old assembly, trodden in the grass, listened to him.
> ' "I'm going to him with this conch in my hands. I'm going to hold it out. Look, I'm goin' to say, you're stronger than I am and you haven't got asthma. You can see, I'm goin' to say, and with both eyes. But I don't ask for my glasses back, not as a favour. I don't ask you to be a sport, I'll say, not because you're strong, but because what's right's right. Give me my glasses, I'm going to say — you got to!" '   (Chapter 11)

But it is too late to appeal to Jack, and Piggy is killed,

92

hurled from the cliff. "Piggy fell forty feet and landed on his back across that square, red rock in the sea. His head opened and stuff came out and turned red. Piggy's arms and legs twitched a bit, like a pig's after it has been killed." Simon, whom Piggy cannot understand, speaks always as the idealist. His faith and courage bring him close to sanctity: his ritual sacrifice is a martyrdom. The other boys think he is mad, and his advice is never heeded because it demands more of them than they can give. The twins, Sam and Eric, who speak antiphonally and act in concert, are types of the ordinary men of good will who do the decent thing as long as possible but eventually succumb to the opposition. They form a benevolent chorus to the action. The other boys are not sharply differentiated. Roger is vicious, Robert and Maurice are of Jack's stamp, but they are not clearly drawn. Nor is the number of boys ever precisely told — we are given a general impression of an island full of boys of various ages from six to twelve. We do not know how many there are, why they are there, or how fast time is passing. They are the common mass on which the leaders work, evasive and idle when the shelters are to be built, neglectful when the fire is to be watched, frightened of the dark and of their elders, but docile and well-disciplined when their faces are painted and they are members of the tribe of Jack's hunters.

A minor difficulty confronting the reader is to know what to make of the ending. In the simple context of the story it comes suddenly and arbitrarily at a time when Ralph is doomed. Since it springs from nothing in the book but comes like the waking out of a nightmare it is hard to attach any symbolic significance to it or to the final irony by which the boys hunting Ralph in fact kindle the fire that leads to rescue. This paradox and the final episode cannot be given a consistent allegorical status, but they may be accepted without strain as part of the narrative. The eye is, as it were, taken away from the microscope at the close, the boys become twelve-year-olds again, and the book ends in the naturalistic mode.

A more serious difficulty in exegesis is to determine how small Mr. Golding's microcosm is, to decide, in other words, whether the island represents a society and the boys the various types and classes in that society, or an individual and the boys the various instincts or promptings in the mind or soul of a man. Although the former is the more obvious view, Mr. Golding does not indicate directly whether one application is intended to exclude the other, and, if so, which is to be preferred. The result is that the reader finds himself called on at intervals to change his focus on the story, to see Jack and Ralph, for instance, now as types of two ways of life, now as opposed impulses or humours in one person. Moreover it is clear that the catastrophe occurs because the qualities of intelligence, address, bravery, decency, organization and insight are divided among Piggy, Jack, Ralph and Simon. Each of them lacks some vital gift: none of them is a complete person. The story has thus on one level unmistakable moral implications for the individual. This blurring of the correspondences necessarily robs the book of the hard satiric edge of, say, *A Tale of a Tub* or *Friendship's Garland*, and of the rigorous personal homiletic power of *The Purple Island* or *The Holy War*. The effect is far more like that of *The Faerie Queene* or *Moby-Dick*, for the symbolism of the novel is not to be completely apprehended by the intellect but exists as a reinforcement and deepening of the story.

The novel thus analyses the disintegration of a group, and the symbolism exposes the desperate wickedness of the human heart: it is evident that the story is grim, its incident macabre, and its overtones, to say the least, not optimistic. Further it must be added that the dominant tone of the book is unsavoury and depressing. When Mr. Golding writes in detail about life on the island it is to emphasise its crudity, and the cruelty and intolerance of the boys, so that his book is painful reading. He makes use of this, however, much as Swift makes use of obscenity. First it helps to convey a sense of truth to life, to break down the Ballantyne picture of life on a tropical island. The diarrhea, the sweat, the pig's blood and the flies are set in powerful contrast to the pastoral life that Ballantyne describes on 'the beautiful, bright, green, coral islands of the Pacific Ocean'. Secondly the emphasis on physical horrors arouses in the reader a physical revulsion from savagery. This is especially true of the pig's head which the hunters leave as a sacrifice to the beast on the mountain, and which in one terrifying episode of delirium takes on the aspect of the Lord of the Flies himself. Thirdly, it demonstrates most remarkably the lengths to which superstitious terror drives the boys, and thus, by implication, the strength of the terror itself. In *Lord of the Flies* indeed superstition is the most powerful agent making for the degeneration of the individual. The book's predominantly wry and unpleasant tone is therefore not a mere flavouring, for in these three ways Mr. Golding makes a vital use of our reactions to dirt and brutality.

The basic procedure in *Lord of the Flies* is the same as that of Mr. Golding's second novel *The Inheritors* — the creation of sympathy for a group which in the face of opposition gradually dissipates. The result is inevitably despair and the disappointment of one hope after another. Thus our compassion for the doomed group is intensified; the deeper our sympathy the greater the force of each successive failure and falling-off. In each book Mr. Golding takes a small group faced with extinction as a symbol of civilization and humanity, but in each his examination leads to a different conclusion. *Lord of the Flies* argues the precariousness of our superiority to beasts and savages, the superficiality of our civilisation, and the impotence of good will and the forms of democracy against the instinctive savagery of man. It thus offers little inducement to optimism. Whereas in *Lord of the Flies* Mr. Golding looks backward and observes how little man has advanced beyond the barbarity of his ancestors, in *The Inheritors*, which deals with the last days of the last of the Neanderthal men, he looks forward from the dawn of history and stresses, following Wells in some detail, the inevitability of the process of natural selection by which True Man has evolved. It may thus be held to imply a wary hopefulness.

There is, I think, a valid criticism that, although no Romantic, Mr. Golding apparently endorses the Romantic fallacy that to examine the *nature* of a thing one must examine it in its most primitive forms. This leads him to use immature societies as his symbols of the community of man. With this reservation, however, it is true to say that he has devised in both books an apposite and original microcosm of humanity, a vehicle admirably fitted to bear the grave tenor of his philosophy. The strongest general criticism of his novels is not that they lack invention but that they lack copiousness. While the island in *Lord of the Flies* and the terrain of *The Inheritors* are acceptable as symbolic theatres of human experience they are not realized in comprehensive and concrete detail. Mr. Golding, that is to say, does not convince as Defoe, for example, convinces, by proliferation of likely circumstance. The opposition in our own times is to Mervyn Peake, whose *Titus Groan* and *Gormenghast* are among the few post-war novels which are not diminished by a comparison with *Lord of the Flies*. Mr. Peake's baroque fertility of incident and detail, his powers of characterization, and his exuberant wit are qualities which Mr. Golding does not match. Instead he works with "strict and adult pen," tidily, economically, and dryly; with the exception before mentioned, he holds his allegory in steady focus, while the symbolic overtones of the Gormenghast books flicker excitingly but elusively beyond definition. Mr. Golding's prose is plain but flexible. He writes sparely in short sentences about the island and the turbulent emotions of the boys, accurately reflecting their limited conversation. Now and then a vivid single word ('a clean flag of flame flying on the mountain', 'the concealing splendours of the sunlight') serves to save him from triteness and to brace the reader for the occasional passages of more complex writing. These occur mainly when he is describing Simon's ordeal and death, as for instance:

> 'Somewhere over the darkened curve of the world the sun and moon were pulling; and the film of water on the earth planet was held, bulging slightly on one side while the solid core turned. The great wave of the tide moved further along the island and the water lifted. Softly, surrounded by a fringe of inquisitive bright creatures, itself a silver shape beneath the steadfast constellations, Simon's dead body moved out towards the open sea.' (Chapter 9.)

Of course the failure to see the island as a whole, and the detached, even callous, descriptions of the successive brutalities are calculated effects of Mr. Golding's narrative method, for he deliberately and skilfully limits his vision to that of the uncomprehending eyes of the boys, recording only what they may be supposed to have seen and felt. This shortening of the field of perception makes immediate the boys' lack of awareness of their own gradual deterioration, a blindness not without its image among men.

96

What I have said so far may convey that Mr. Golding's novels in general and *Lord of the Flies* in particular are rather depressing books, arousing but not purging our terror and pity, and bedevilled with allegorical equivalences which carry, on the whole, pessimistic implications. No doubt there are those who find that reading Swift lowers their nervous tone. To these *Lord of the Flies* cannot be recommended. But for those who are prepared to learn even from so astringent and sceptical a tutor as Mr. Golding it is possible to find in his work lessons not merely negative. Both his novels stress, and the second pivots on, the theme of communication. In each he isolates a society which is destroyed largely because its members cannot adequately express their thoughts either to themselves or to one another. Two quotations from critical points in *Lord of the Flies* serve to illustrate the importance of the theme.

> 'They [Ralph and Jack] walked along, two continents of experience and feeling, unable to communicate.
> ' "If I could only get a pig!"
> ' "I'll come back and go on with the shelter."
> 'They looked at each other, baffled, in love and hate.' (Chapter 3.)

> 'The two boys [Ralph and Jack] faced each other. There was the brilliant world of hunting, tactics, fierce exhilaration, skill; and there was the world of longing and baffled common-sense.' (Chapter 4.)

It is not irrelevant to observe that much of *Lord of the Flies* is taken up with accounts of the assemblies and the attempts of Ralph, Piggy and Simon to make articulate and acceptable their pictures of what the boys must do to be saved. Man, therefore, cannot raise himself except in concert with other men. But from this, still without making Mr. Golding an optimist, we may reasonably infer that if men do in fact understand one another there is some hope that they may live a better life and achieve a more stable civilization. Of mutual comprehension, indeed, one feels that Mr. Golding would say what the scarred pirate in *The Coral Island* said of the Gospel:

> '... I know that when any o' the islands chance
> to get it, trade goes all smooth an' easy; but where
> they ha'nt got it, Beelzebub himself could hardly
> desire better company.' (Chapter 23.)

In *The Coral Island* Beelzebub, the Lord of the Flies, finds his congenial prey in the unconverted natives. Mr. Golding is less ready to divide the races of man. He writes more densely and more compactly than Ballantyne, combining in one island and one community, perhaps in one person the impulses Ballantyne separates and distributes appropriately between the savages and the manly British lads.

For since the book moves, as people live, on two levels, the individual and the social, what is true to Mr. Golding of communication in a society is true also of individual self-knowledge and freedom from superstition, especially from the kind of unreasoning terror which takes shape in the book as the Lord of the Flies. Simon's peculiar strength is that he is not frightened of the island. Such a state of grace is not possible to all men, but there is hope in Ralph's gradual development to maturity. Although he is on the point of defeat when the cruiser arrives, he has learned steadily throughout the book. He learns to recognize the quality of Piggy's mind, to understand the minds of his enemies, to notice how far short he falls of his own standards, to think, to make rapid decisions, to realize that the rules must be obeyed 'because the rules are the only things we've got'. Like Lok in *The Inheritors* he grows by discovering more about himself and his fellows, but especially about himself.

Lord of the Flies, for all its clarity of outline, is a complex novel. Although it is immediately successful simply as narrative it draws its distinguishing power from its value as a symbolic representation. That is to say it is a parable whose truth must be recognized, not discovered intellectually, a sustained metaphor for human experience, for 'the end of innocence, the darkness of man's heart'.

Review of Criticism

Although *Lord of the Flies* is a recent novel, it has already become the battleground for a number of critics, all of whom urge their own reading of the novel, and who are also sniping at each other. For some reason this book invites controversy. Perhaps the reason has to do with the utterly convincing quality of the narrative itself. It seems so real that readers, succumbing to the magic of Golding's style, fall into the illusion that they are talking about real boys. Certainly, the story invites analysis both as a means of understanding the fictional tale and as a means of understanding ourselves. At any rate, it is worthwhile to read as many critical comments as possible, for each contributes further to a total understanding of this complex piece of writing.

Frank Kermode

Kermode, comparing *Lord of the Flies* to Ballantyne's *The Coral Island*, writes satirically of the high place Ballantyne accords British imperialistic and colonizing attitudes of the 19th century. Golding, says Kermode, is a "darker" writer but a much truer one, and a far more skilful one. Kermode stresses the rather modern concept that civilized man — not the savages — is corrupt. Golding's boys, he suggests, would ruin the simple savages. This point of view contrasts with *The Coral Island* where the savages are cannibals and the boys are

> cleanly (cold baths recommended) and godly — regenerate, empire building boys, who know by instinct how to turn paradise into a British protectorate.

Unlike John Peter, Kermode sees Simon's death as accidental. The boys "mistake" Simon for the beast and kill him.

> As Piggy, the dull, practical intelligence, is reduced to blindness and futility, so Simon, the visionary, is murdered before he can communicate his comfortable knowledge.

Kermode relates the novel to the real world by defining it

in terms of two cultures, the followers of Jack or the admirers of Simon:

> Those who build fortresses and those who want to name the beast.

Kermode stresses the critic's right to interpret the work of art as he sees fit. He says the artist may even be "wrong" about what he means in his writing. Thus, Kermode denies that the dead parachutist is "history," as Golding himself says it is. Kermode feels this meaning was not successfully communicated, but that the airman becomes a mythic figure of even greater importance than it would be if seen merely as a symbol of history.

Carl Niemeyer

Niemeyer presents a fairly detailed comparison of *The Coral Island* and *Lord of the Flies*. According to Niemeyer, Golding finds evil in the boys' own natures, not in the outside world, as Ballantyne does. For example, the pirates of Ballantyne's book are evil forces which intrude upon the boys' island paradise. They are "white men who have renounced or scorned their Christian heritage." By a simple inversion of causal sequence, their renunciation of Christianity makes them pirates, for they are outside of the Christian society, the morally lawful society, and therefore *are* pirates. Ballantyne's uncritical optimism is shown in that the cannibals who threaten the boys:

> ... undergo an unmotivated conversion to Christianity which effects a total change in their nature just in time to rescue the boys from their clutches.

Niemeyer finds Ralph, the leader, and Piggy, the braintrust, "incomplete" as persons, and Simon's failure is "the inevitable failure of the mystic — what he knows is beyond words." And the larger theme of the novel is seen in Jack:

> Jack stands for naked ruthless power, the police force or the military force acting without restraint

and gradually absorbing the whole state into itself
and annihilating what it cannot absorb.

Niemeyer concludes that *The Coral Island* is a book of blacks and whites, simple contests between good and evil. But he finds Golding's book a symbolic one, in which it is shown that only civilization keeps at bay the "beast" in men.

John Peter

Peter distinguishes between two art forms: the fable and the fiction. He defines a fable as written so as to suggest that the conclusions to be drawn from it have already been foreseen by the author. The artist is writing in such a way as to cause the conclusion to come about as he wants it to. Fiction, on the other hand, is defined as writing in which whatever conclusions are to be drawn come out of the story, the fiction itself, and are not anterior to the writing. That is, they were not foreseen by the author in such a way as to cause him to write his story around the idea of eventually reaching certain conclusions. Fable begins with a "skeletal abstract" which the writer tries to endow with life. *Lord of the Flies*, Peter says, is such a fable. In contrast, the fiction begins with flesh and blood situations and characters out of which the writer tries to arrive at an understanding.

Peter concentrates his attention upon Simon in his analysis of the novel as a fable. Unlike Kermode, he believes that the boys knew what they were doing when they killed Simon, for he says that Simon is a "more or less intentional sacrifice." But, on the character of Simon, Peter is dissatisfied. He finds the devices of fable overdone and thus unsuccessful. Simon's saying of the beast, "Maybe it's only us," and his vision of the beast as "a human at once heroic and sick" are pointed out as weaknesses. They are really editorializing comments by the author, and not part of the story:

This over-explicitness is my main criticism of what
is in many ways a work of real distinction.

Golding seems to use Simon as a mouthpiece for his own ideas, and excuses the device by means of Simon's mystical character, but Peter finds the character of Simon unconvincing:

Some warrant is provided for this clairvoyance in Simon's mysterious illness, but it is inadequate. The boy remains unconvincing in himself, and his presence constitutes a standing invitation to the author to avoid the trickiest problems of his method, by commenting too baldly on the issues he has raised.

Of the fable itself, Peter says that the boys' society

represents, in embryo, the society of the adult world, their impulses and convictions are those of adults incisively abridged, and the whole narrative is a powerfully ironic commentary on the nature of Man, an accusation levelled at us all.

Of the beast, Peter says that it is

... Beelzebub, Lord of the Flies, Roger and Jack and you and I, ready to declare himself as soon as we permit him to.

Peter sees the dead parachutist as "man himself, the boys' own natures, the something that all humans have in common."

Ian Gregor and Mark Kinkead-Weekes

These authors agree that *Lord of the Flies* is a fable, but insist that it is simultaneously a fiction. They observe that the symbolic references such as those to trees with both flowers and fruit, or to *The Coral Island*, are only successful because the novel is successful as a fiction:

The sun and thunder come across to us as physical realities, not because they have a symbolic part to play in the book, but because of the novelist's superb resourcefulness of language.

The book is important, according to these authors, because it fulfils the basic requisite of art: that of showing the reader a picture with which he can identify:

... Mr. Golding's book is valuable to us, not because it *"tells us about"* the darkness of man's heart, but because it shows it, because it is a work of art which enables us to enter into the world it creates and live at the level of a deeply perceptive and intelligent man.

The writers do agree that "the darkness of man's heart" that Ralph came to understand is the subject of the book, and add:

It is worth remembering that this book, published in 1954, was written in a world very different from Ballantyne's, one which had seen within twenty years the systematic destruction of the Jewish race, a world war revealing unnumbered atrocities of what man had done to man, and in 1945 the mushroom cloud of the atomic bomb which has come to dominate all our political and moral thinking.

William R. Mueller

Mueller asserts that *Lord of the Flies* is carefully organized around six hunts, and that each hunt carries us closer to "man's essential core." This "core" is presented as being consonant with the Christian position that man is a "fallen creature" who is guilty of Original Sin and therefore is by nature sinful. Thus, the novel is seen as an "old story" in that it follows the Judeo-Christian tradition which holds that man is an ignoble creature, expelled from paradise for the sin of disobedience. As the boys gradually get over their awe at the sight of blood, their taste for killing intensifies. After the first kill, Jack "twitched" when retelling of his exploit. But by the fourth hunt (the killing of the sow), the boys feel "no twitch of conscience, no element of pretence." The fifth hunt, during which Simon is killed, moves us "even closer to the unbridled impulses of the human heart." And the sixth hunt (which is for Ralph's head) represents the final depravity of fallen man: cannibalism.

Mueller reinforces his theological reading of the book by identifying the Lord of the Flies as Beelzebub, called in Luke

11:15 "the chief of the devils." Thus, the principle of evil is intended, according to Mueller, as the meaning behind the beast:

> He is the demonic essence whose inordinate hunger, never assuaged, seeks to devour all men, to bend them to his will.

The intention of the book, says Mueller, is not only to terrify, by showing man as endlessly perpetrating evil, but also to show through Simon the importance of recognizing the evil principle as a means of getting rid of it. This "saving recognition," according to Mueller, is the "conviction of sin" which man must face:

> The novel is the parable of fallen man. But it does not close the door on that man; it entreats him to know himself and his Adversary, for he cannot do combat against an unrecognized force, especially when it lies within him.

Claire Rosenfield

Rosenfield claims that Golding consciously set out to dramatize Freudian theory. She recognizes the imagery surrounding Ralph and Jack as being godlike and satanic:

> These two are very obviously intended to recall God and the Devil . . . but as Freud reminds us, "metaphysics" becomes "metapsychology"; gods and devils are "nothing other than the processes projected into the outer world." If Ralph is a projection of man's good impulses from which we derive the authority figures — whether god, king, or father — who establish the necessity for our valid ethical and social action, then Jack becomes an externalization of the evil instinctual forces of the unconscious; the allegorical has become the psychological.

From this point of view, Piggy's physical description is intended to place him in the role of an authority figure, a father, one who urges common sense, and therefore spoils the element of "play" by constantly returning the children to the real world by interrupting their world of illusions. When the play becomes real enough, he will be killed, because he is spoiling the "game." But it's not really a game at all:

> Ironically, the child of *Lord of the Flies* who thinks he is "only pretending" or that this is "only for fun" does not realize that his play is the beginning of the formation of a new society which has regressed to a primitive state, with all its emphasis upon taboo and communal action. What begins by being like other games in having a distinct "locality and duration" apart from ordinary life is — or becomes — reality.

The ritual that follows the killing of the first pig, for example, is a "game" played to reassure the boys that the terrible deed of killing, shedding blood, is not for real; it is only "pretend." But identification begins to occur:

> Each time they re-enact the same event, however, their behavior becomes more frenzied, more cruel, less like dramatization or imitation than identification.

The same is true of the taboo that evolves from the absence of parents to tell the children what to do and what not to do:

> Ralph now uses Jack's name with the recognition that "a taboo was evolving around that word too." Name and thing again become one; to use the word is to incite the bearer, who is not here a transcendent or supernatural creature but rather a small boy. But more significant, the taboo, according to Freud, is "a very primitive prohibition imposed from without [by an authority] and directed against the strongest desires of man."

Rosenfield traces many elements of the novel to mythology. Thus, she recalls that the bringing of fire to man marked the beginning of civilization — and of its accompanying forms of repression — all of which is caught up in the use made of Piggy's glasses. His loss of sight, from this point of view, marks the gradual loss of repression and the consequent emergence of the boys into irrationality.

Rosenfield finds in mythology a source for Simon's illusion, just as he fainted, that he was "inside the mouth" of the Lord of the Flies:

> Mythologically and symbolically it recalls the quest in which the hero is swallowed by a serpent or dragon or beast whose belly represents the underworld, undergoes a ritual death in order to win the elixir to revitalize his stricken society, and returns with his knowledge to the timed world as a redeemer.... Psychologically this ... represents the annihilation of the individual ego, an internal journey, necessary for self-understanding, a return from the timelessness of the unconscious.

E.L. Epstein

Epstein sees Wiliam Golding's achievement as his having

> combined and synthesized all of the characteristically twentieth-century methods of analysis of the human being and human society and used this unified knowledge to comment on a "test situation." In this book, as in few others at the present time, are findings of psychoanalysts of all schools, anthropologists, social psychologists and philosophical historians mobilized into an attack upon the central problem of modern thought: the nature of the human personality and the reflection of personality upon society.

Epstein specifically denies that the Lord of the Flies is to be mistaken for any mythical or supernatural devil; but sees it much as Rosenfield does:

> He does not, of course, suggest that the Devil is present in any traditional religious sense; Golding's Beelzebub is the modern equivalent, the anarchic,

amoral, driving Id whose only function seems to be to insure the survival of the host in which it is embedded or embodied, which function it performs with tremendous and single-minded tenacity.

As mentioned earlier in the chapter on meaning, Epstein offers a Freudian reading of the novel in Oedipal terms, and sees the killing of the sow as signalling the emergence of childhood sexual experience as it is played out in what amounts to a symbolic rape of the sow.

Bibliography

BABB, HOWARD S., *The Novels of William Golding*, Columbus: Ohio State University Press, 1970.

BAKER, JAMES R., "Why It's No Go," *Arizona Quarterly*, 19 (Winter, 1963), 293-305.

_____ , *William Golding: A Critical Study*, New York: St. Martin's Press, 1965.

COX, C.B. *"Lord of the Flies,"* *Critical Quarterly*, II (1960), 112-117.

DICK, BERNARD F., *William Golding*, New York: Twayne, 1967.

EPSTEIN, E.L., "Notes on *Lord of the Flies*," *Lord of the Flies*, Capricorn Books, 1959.

GINDIN, JAMES, " 'Gimmick' and Metaphor in the Novels of William Golding," *Modern Fiction Studies*, 6 (Summer, 1960), 145-52. Reprinted in Gindin's *Postwar British Fiction*, University of California Press, 1962.

GREGOR, IAN and MARK KINKEAD-WEEKES, "Introduction," *Lord of the Flies*, London: Faber and Faber School Editions, 1962.

HODSON, LEIGHTON, *William Golding*, Edinburgh: Oliver and Boyd, 1969.

HYNES, SAMUEL, *William Golding*, New York: Columbia University Press, 1964.

KERMODE, FRANK, "Coral Island," *The Spectator*, CCI (August 22, 1958), 257.

―――, and WILLIAM GOLDING, "The Meaning of it All," *Books and Bookmen*, 5 (October 1959), 9-10.

―――, "The Novels of William Golding," *International Literary Annual*, III (1961), 11-29.

"Lord of the Campus," *Time*, 79 (June 22, 1962), 64.

MUELLER, WILLIAM R., "An Old Story Well Told," *Christian Century*, 80 (October 2, 1963), 1203-06.

NELSON, WILLIAM, ed., *William Golding's 'Lord of the Flies,' A Source Book*, New York: Odyssey Press, 1963.

NIEMEYER, CARL, "The Coral Island Revisited," *College English*, 22 (January, 1961), 241-45.

OLDSEY, BERNARD S. and STANLEY WEINTRAUB, *The Art of William Golding*, New York: Harcourt, Brace and World, 1965.

PETER, JOHN, "The Fables of William Golding," *Kenyon Review*, 19 (Autumn, 1957), 577-92.

PRITCHETT, V.S., "Secret Parables," *New Statesman* (August 2, 1958), 146-47.

ROSENFIELD, CLAIRE, "Men of a Smaller Growth: A Psychological Analysis of William Golding's *Lord of the Flies,*" *Literature and Psychology*, 11 (Autumn 1961), 93-101.

TIGER, VIRGINIA M., *William Golding: The Dark Fields of Discovery*, London: Calder & Boyars, 1974.

WALTERS, MARGARET, "Two Fabulists: Golding and Camus," *Melbourne Critical Review*, No. 4 (1961), 18-29.

WHITE, ROBERT J., "Butterfly and Beast in *Lord of the Flies,*" *Modern Fiction Studies*, X (Summer, 1964), 163-70.